"Wouldn't you know it! I wa[...] fruit of the Spirit showing [...] Kristin's book has been on my desk for weeks. I 'just happened' to grab it during a moment when I was trying to catch my breath during a super-busy day. BAM! I couldn't put it down! The right book at the right time! The other stuff can wait. *Deep Roots, Good Fruit* is filled with Scripture-saturated encouragement. Kristin has a gift for pairing observation with inspiration. She makes me want to be more like Jesus. Thanks Kristin!"

Kurt Goff, Host, Kurt and Kate Mornings, Moody Radio

"If Kristin Couch had only helped me to better understand the fruit of the Spirit, I would be grateful. But this book does far more; through brilliant storytelling, Couch makes the Spirit's fruit smellable, tasteable, and alluringly beautiful."

Scott Hubbard, Editor, Desiring God (desiringgod.org)

"It is one of God's greatest promises and one of our foremost encouragements: that he is changing us from the inside out. By the work of his Spirit, he is transforming us so we bear fruit—fruit that displays the goodness and grace of our Savior. That is the subject of this book, which has been written by one of my favorite authors. And as Kristin does on her blog and elsewhere, she not only writes what is true, but she writes it beautifully and compellingly."

Tim Challies, Author, Seasons of Sorrow

"*Deep Roots, Good Fruit* puts what matters most into plain sight through vivid storytelling. You will walk away feeling encouraged, inspired and convicted, and ultimately desiring to be more like Christ through the power of his Spirit."

Lyndsay Keith, Host, Centerpoint, TBN

"Kristin Couch's book is a wonderful resource to emphasis the necessity of the Spirit's work in believers' lives. More than just teaching about the fruit of the Spirit, Kristin has given us real-life examples of what that looks like in everyday life. I highly recommend it."

Pastor Bryant Crane, Church Planter, George, South Africa

"*Deep Roots, Good Fruit* is like medicine for a dry and weary soul. When Kristin writes, it is like a brush on canvas that makes you see so vividly what she intends. How she uses her own stories to paint the picture of what the precious Holy Spirit has given to us through the fruit of the Spirit is certainly encouraging and simply refreshing."

Brian McDougall, Executive Pastor, Idlewild Baptist Church, Lutz, Florida

"In a world where 'spiritual amnesia' has infiltrated our hearts and minds, *Deep Roots, Good Fruit* brings us back to the truth of God's word and the reminder that the Holy Spirit is willing and available to us at any moment of need to give us the desire, power, and ability to accomplish his will. I highly recommend this book to anyone who needs encouragement and the reminder of God's love and care for us. *Deep Roots, Good Fruit* was a huge encouragement to me as it focused on the fruit of the Spirit. Several words came to mind as I read this. *Biblical*: it never strayed from the truth. *Authentic*: it's obvious these were not just words on a page but life-changing words from someone who has experienced them. *Encouraging*: from beginning to end—and a reminder of the power of the Spirit to change and transform lives, including mine. Thank you, Kristin, for your transparency and authenticity in *Deep Roots, Good Fruit*."

John Myers, Director of Ministry Advancement, Strategic Renewal

"Growth in godliness is slow, and it's easy to become discouraged. In this beautifully written book, Kristin Couch skilfully weaves story and Scripture together to show how God's Spirit works, gently and patiently, through the day-to-day, seemingly insignificant experiences of life to grow good fruit in his people. Her invitation to slow down and notice this transforming work in your own life will encourage you and fuel your desire to grow more like Jesus."

Carolyn Lacey, Author, Say the Right Thing *and*
Extraordinary Hospitality (for Ordinary People)

Deep Roots

Good Fruit

Seeing the
Fruit of the
Spirit through
Story & Scripture

Kristin
Elizabeth
Couch

Deep Roots, Good Fruit
© Kristin Elizabeth Couch, 2024.

Published by:
The Good Book Company

thegoodbook.com | thegoodbook.co.uk
thegoodbook.com.au | thegoodbook.co.nz | thegoodbook.co.in

ISBN: 9781802541090 | JOB-007698 | Printed in Turkey

Design by Drew McCall

The earth was without form and void, and darkness was over the face of the deep. And the Spirit of God was hovering over the face of the waters.

Genesis 1:2

Abide in me, and I in you. As the branch cannot bear fruit by itself, unless it abides in the vine, neither can you, unless you abide in me. I am the vine; you are the branches. Whoever abides in me and I in him, he it is that bears much fruit, for apart from me you can do nothing.

John 15:4–5

For my godly husband, Jon, and our beloved children:
Caleb, Jacob, Marcus, and Lauren.

As our family tree flourishes through marriage, I am
happy to also dedicate my words to Natalia, Taryn,
and Alexander.

And for CJ, our first grandchild, who prizes trucks
and good books.

You are a gift, my sweet boy. May you grow up into
Christ, with deep roots bearing good fruit.

CONTENTS

INTRODUCTION

Under New Ownership

When my husband and I first glimpsed the house that would become our new home, we instantly fell in love. There it sat: resplendent, perched at the end of a long driveway, with a luscious lawn stretching before it. It was clear that spring rains had recently been at work: waves of verdant grass sloped endlessly over the front yard.

Once inside the house, we ambled through every nook with our realtor. Opening cupboards and closets, we gazed at each room from varied angles, as our imaginations soared. We pictured our grown children and grandchildren in *this* room and *that* room—visions of delightfully boisterous holiday dinners, the fireplace roaring on those dark and frigid winter evenings.

By the time we stepped off the front steps and into the front yard, I had splendid notions swirling in my head. It was then that I noticed my husband quietly studying the lawn.

He turned to me.

"This isn't grass at all, only bright weeds."

Weeds that were multiplying by the day, as it turned out, filling much of the yard. The previous owners had opted to forego yard maintenance—other than occasionally running a lawn mower over the invasive undergrowth. While it looked both tamed and vibrant from a distance, at close range it was obvious that the yard was diseased.

We purchased this lovely home anyway. And once we had signed on the dotted line and the keys were ours, we grabbed our work gloves and rolled up our sleeves. We quickly discovered that ridding weeds with the hope of growing a healthy yard is a slow, costly labor. But we were determined to transform that yard into everything we knew it could become.

Several years have elapsed, and the front lawn has been transformed. Plush, thick grass is now abounding. As our grandson runs barefoot, I am grateful for the new health of our yard, gently soft and inviting.

Weeds still pop up occasionally, and my husband plucks them up by the roots. We do so for the love of our property, our family, and our neighbors. As the yard's health continues to flourish, it is a pleasure to invite others to enjoy it with us, or to sit out there alone in the sunshine with a good book. A lush, green lawn is a splendid gift to enjoy.

It's a wonder what a change of ownership can do.

One of the most encouraging ideas of the New Testament is that God wants to work a similar transformation in us. When we become Christians, our souls come under new ownership. We have been transferred from the kingdom of darkness into the kingdom of light (Colossians 1:13). And now it's as though God dons his gloves, rolls up his sleeves, and gets to work, restoring life and beauty to the home he has set his love upon.

And how does he do this?

Through the Holy Spirit.

But who is he? There is an air of mystery surrounding our triune, three-in-one God. Our finite minds cannot begin to fathom how God the Father, Jesus Christ the Son, and the Holy Spirit are distinct Persons, yet one God. Often, it is our love for the Holy Spirit that is most neglected, and our understanding of him sadly remains hazy .

Yet the Holy Spirit is God, first introduced to us all the way back in Genesis 1:

> *The earth was without form and void, and darkness was over the face of the deep. And the Spirit of God was hovering over the face of the waters.*
>
> *(Genesis 1:2)*

The same Spirit who brought creation to life now dwells within the heart of every Christ-follower: "Do you not know," writes the apostle Paul to the wayward Christians of Corinth, "that you are God's temple and that God's Spirit dwells in you?" (1 Corinthians 3:16).

Our triune God has chosen to make us his dwelling place. Think of it—our Holy God is now living and breathing within our feeble frames. What an immeasurable gift!

Yet perhaps, as you open up this book, you're feeling as I often do: discouraged by your lack of progress in bearing spiritual fruit, overwhelmed by your persistent sin struggles, or grieved by the sense of spiritual apathy that creeps upon you as God seems distant.

I assure you that God is not distant, but present, and working on your behalf. It is my prayer, as you travel through the pages of this book, that your affection for the Holy Spirit will deepen and flourish as he first grows, then ripens, his fruit within you. He is your Teacher, Comforter, Leader, and Guide—your God who resides within you, growing you in sanctification and making you more like Jesus.

Your sinful, weed-infested yard is under new ownership. The tangled, shabby growth has been replaced by good soil, nourishing the fruit trees in your yard—tiny trees that, given time, will grow tall and sturdy, and produce bright and healthy fruit that brings glory to God. As Jesus said, "By this my father is glorified, that you bear much fruit and so prove to be my disciples" (John 15:8).

So what exactly does a fruitful life look like? The apostle Paul handed the church of Galatia a stunning list of godly traits meant to dance and sparkle within the lives of believers:

> *The fruit of the Spirit is love, joy, peace, patience, kindness, goodness, faithfulness, gentleness, self-control. (Galatians 5:22-23)*

Do not misunderstand: this is not a checklist of traits to drum up with the hopes of receiving heavenly merit. Rather, these traits are the identifying characteristics of a Christian, produced by the Holy Spirit. They give credence to our conversion. And often they are right there, slowly growing, if we have eyes to see them.

So I invite you to see firsthand the fruit of the Holy Spirit blossoming in these quiet stories from my ordinary life, and reflect on how he is working in yours. I like to imagine myself as a treasure hunter, turning over stories from my past, and sifting through life's mundane moments for marks of the divine. The Spirit's work appears in the margins—in life's crevices with common people.

May this book encourage you to view your days and stories through the lens of Scripture. God is always working and he is always good. Trust him and watch your spiritual fruit gradually flourish. Just as our healthy lawn took years to become vibrant, growing grass, so it is with spiritual fruit—it takes time and attention to mature.

So come along with me as we explore *love, joy, peace, patience, kindness, goodness, faithfulness, gentleness, and self-control* through story and God's word. (You'll also find reflection questions for each chapter at the end of the book.) My hope is that as you meditate on these attributes, you will long for them more deeply, pray for them more fervently, and catch increasing glimpses of them in your own life and the lives of believers you love.

> *If we live by the Spirit, let us also keep in step with the Spirit. (Galatians 5:25)*

ONE

Love: A Heart that Gives

"For God so loved the world that he gave…"
(John 3:16)

One warm summer's day, when I was nine, our family drove to the city to meet relatives and their friends for a festival. I skipped along the crowded sidewalk, eager to meet a certain little boy, Joel, whom I had heard so much about.

As we approached our meeting place, my parents admonished me: *Be polite and don't stare! Remember that he looks different from everyone else.*

I was ill-prepared.

~

A handful of years earlier, on a crisp September morning, a father leaned out the car window, smiling as he paid the toll-booth fee. His young family was excited to embark on a much-needed vacation.

Without warning, a semi-trailer truck barreled full speed into the back of their car, which burst into flames. They scrambled out of the vehicle, dazed and burned— except for their handsome blond-headed toddler, Joel, who remained strapped to his car seat, tethered inside the inferno.

A stranger, who had witnessed the entire horror, heard the baby's screams and with no thought for his own welfare reached inside the burning vehicle and yanked the little boy and his car seat out of the blaze.

Joel had melted into the plastic. He was now charred beyond recognition, and was nearly dead. Skin dripped off of his tiny body and pooled beneath him as everyone waited for medics to arrive.

To the astonishment of doctors and nurses, Joel lived. They had never seen a case this dire end in *life*.

As we approached Joel and his father, waiting for us in the middle of the bustling festival, my heart sank. Joel's father held him high, perched tall upon his shoulders. This little fellow peered from a face utterly marred beyond any former recognition. He had suffered third-degree burns on over 85% of his body. After his fingers had fallen off, surgeons created a lobster-like claw-hand. Skin grafts had created a mask-like appearance about his face. His mouth was stretched tight and shaped in a perfectly surprised "O"—the size of a Cheerio.

I looked away, mindful not to stare. Even as I did so, children passed by in the crowd, pointing, jeering, and uttering cruelties quite impossible to ignore. One boy even shrieked: *He looks like a monkey!* The boy's parents gaped at Joel before they hushed their child and moved along with the surging crowd, offering no apology.

It was agonizing to watch.

Joel's father smiled broadly at my brother and me, nonplussed. "This is Joel," he said. I waved and then blushed, realizing that he could not wave back.

"Joel loves when people say 'hi!'" he encouraged. And then, "Wow! It's hot! Let's find an ice-cream stand."

So we did. I followed behind this small fellow perched so high upon his father's shoulders, overhearing snippets of sentences from father to son, "Such a gorgeous day," and, "God made the sun and clouds and trees."

His words were gentle and kind.

This giant of a man, literally and figuratively, swelled with untamed love for his boy. He was utterly undeterred by the stares of strangers. Their curiosity and insults could not chink his armor.

I studied this father's sturdiness in those few hours we spent together. Never once did he retort, glare, or turn sour. He loved not only Joel but others, including my brother and me. Joel's father had eyes to see that my brother and I were like Joel—hot and hungry little people, longing for some sweet, cold ice cream.

We soon happened upon a soft-serve stand and ordered.

I was curious—how could this little boy eat?

His father eased him down from his shoulders, gently placing him in a stroller. And then, taking the top of the ice cream into his own mouth he created a thin, pencil-shaped tip to the soft-serve, placing the sliver into Joel's tiny, eager mouth.

And this is how he proceeded to share the entire cone with his boy. It singed my memory—the most majestic act of love that I have ever seen. Patient and joyful, he laughed as Joel consumed the delicious dessert, little by little. He praised his son, speaking serene words that solidified a gloriously normal activity. The moment was intimate and poignant—a sacrifice of time, done in the knowledge that this son of his would likely never be able to give back in conventional ways.

Yet even as he did so, Joel's father engaged us in conversation, asking about our lives. How much easier it would have been for him to focus on Joel or even himself! Yet by continually focusing on others, he gave his disabled son not just an ice cream, but a model of Christ-like love.

If I close my eyes now, I can picture my little girl-self mentally comparing the differences between this father's affections and those with which I was most familiar, a tender scale within my small hands. I felt a distinct pang—a longing for more. A wishful desire for everyday conversation about God, for surging displays of both affection and purpose, for the tenderness of this father-child relationship.

I actually felt more sorrow for the bratty boy who had behaved atrociously, calling Joel a monkey, than I did for this little disfigured Joel. If anything, it was Joel to be envied, with such a father lifting him heavenward, high above the broken fray. This father was giving of himself, moment by moment, mouthful by mouthful, day by day. I watched, transfixed.

Such love seemed ethereal.

The word *love* seems elusive, difficult to define, doesn't it? It is challenging to disentangle culture's version of love from that of our heavenly Father.

The world often associates love with something to be taken. It is equated with a strong feeling, a passing emotion, a whim: grabbing what you desperately desire. Pair that with our flippant overuse of the word, and no wonder we have misplaced the keys to truth.

*I **love** this sandwich.*
*I **love** autumn.*
*I **love** your haircut.*
*I **love** God.*

How confusing it is to use *love* to express fondness for anything and everything. We must begin afresh. With God's word.

1 John 4:7-8 states:

> *Beloved, let us love one another, for love is from God, and whoever loves has been born of God and knows God. Anyone who does not love does not know God, because God is love.*

God is the perfect Author of love, its Creator! It starts at the very center of his being. "God is love" because God is Trinity: Father, Son, and Holy Spirit, existing forever in self-giving relationships of love; delighting in one another from before the beginning of time. Before anything else came into existence—before any star or planet, before any amoeba or maple tree, owl or chipmunk, before one second of human history had passed—God *loved*.

This is a love God could have kept to himself. And yet he didn't.

First, he made us. We are people fashioned in his image. Think of it! Creatures of dust and rib, loved by God himself.

And then, he saved us. John 3:16 tells us:

> *For God so loved the world, that he gave his only*
> *Son, that whoever believes in him should not perish,*
> *but have eternal life.*

God gave what was most precious—the life of his Son. Our heavenly Father not only gifts us with breath in our lungs but true spiritual life in our hearts, in order that we might live in his presence for all of eternity. It cost him everything, and yet he did not waver, because of his gracious, expansive love for us, his children by faith. Love *gives sacrificially*, and always for the good of others.

And yet what makes God's love all the more astonishing is who he chooses to bestow it on. God loved "the world"—a world in rebellion against him.

This is what I know: Joel's father loved his boy in a way that made my heart long for such tender, sacrificial love. He was an unattractive little boy: scarred, burned, disfigured, and yet beautiful and precious in his father's eyes.

Isn't that the perfect picture?

We are neither lovely nor flawless, but fallen human beings with sins and scars and shame. Yet in Christ, we are cherished, loved, and kept for eternity—lifted high and held secure, like a child upon a father's shoulders. Our name is etched in the book of life. Nothing can take away his love for us. What more could we ever need?

I longed to be loved like Joel was, and the truth of it is, *I am*. And by faith in Christ, so are you.

As we press into such thoughts, lingering there, it is clear to see how such generosity gifted by God naturally results in an overflow of love for others, just as Joel's father modeled for our family. He was free to love sacrificially, because he knew that he was loved by God in this same way. As John goes on to say in his first letter:

> *In this is love, not that we have loved God but that he loved us and sent his Son to be the propitiation for our sins. Beloved, if God so loved us, we also ought to love one another. (1 John 4:10-11)*

May we be joyful imitators, mirroring the love of our heavenly Father through sacrificial giving in small, daily measures.

How do we arrive at the extraordinary heart-posture of Joel's father, which displayed the unmistakable imprint of such godly love? May I suggest that we begin afresh, in this moment called *today*.

It bears repeating: love is not based upon a feeling. Pastor John MacArthur defines love as "a determined act of the will, which always results in determined acts of self-giving. Love is the willing, joyful desire to put the welfare of others above our own" (The MacArthur New Testament Commentary on 1 Corinthians 13). Our emotions are natural and a good gift from God, but they are not meant to rule over our will. When God told Israel to love him with all of their heart, soul, mind, and strength (Deuteronomy 6:5), he was instructing them to love him fully, with every fiber of their being.

When my husband and I were raising our four children, the day to day training fell to me, as my husband was working to provide for our family. There were many days when affection for my children sprang naturally from my heart. But there were other times when I simply did not feel like serving them, disciplining them, and placing my children's needs before my own. It did not matter. I had committed myself to loving my precious children sacrificially, my life for their lives. This settled conviction then served to steer my emotions. I made many mistakes, as a sinful woman, but it was that act of the will that brought my emotions limping into eventual submission. Very often, feelings of love follow where acts of love lead.

If we are cooperating with the Holy Spirit, he is already making us more like Christ, and stirring in us a longing to love others well.

So consider the day ahead. How could you start giving yourself away for the good of others in some small way— tender givings that may yield a large impact? Often we daydream of grand, sweeping gestures to amaze others. Yet it is often small kindnesses that most clearly herald love.

I know someone who randomly surprises his coworkers with their favorite coffee orders and a box of bagels each month. He does not have extra money, but chooses to cheerfully go without certain comforts in order to bless others, understanding that everything he has truly belongs to God. His joy is in the giving, as he stewards resources with eternity in mind.

It could be as simple as emptying the dishwasher without being asked, or raking leaves for a neighbor. Or graciously listening to the lonely and long-winded storyteller at church whom no one else will patiently engage with.

As we do these things over and over again, little by little, day by day, we learn to love others as God loves us.

Think about a time when you felt deeply loved. I would venture to say it involved someone going out of their way to perform a kindness, something which went above the humdrum pattern of normal life. It probably cost that individual something to love you well: time, money, or their own personal preferences.

> *Little children, let us not love in word or talk but in deed and in truth. (1 John 3:18)*

My husband is a pastor—a servant. I watch him give and give and give some more. Sadly, pastors are often taken for granted, serving as a means to someone's end. Many forget that pastors are *real* people.

Recently, we were invited to a church person's home for dinner, a family we did not know well. Upon entering, I was enveloped by the fine aroma of chicken pasta. Our host had set the table pretty as classical music swirled in the background. The husband beckoned us inside, as his wife placed the finishing touches on our feast.

Soon we sat down and prayed a blessing. The food was delicious. Later, we were presented with dessert: a tall berry trifle, layered in a lovely glass bowl. The whipped cream pudding mixture, bedded with cake and berries, was tasty. This entire feast had certainly taken our hosts hours to prepare. We were simply the grateful recipients.

This act of hospitality was not performed out of drudgery, but love. It wasn't flashy but their sacrifice of time and money and tender attention to detail produced a welcoming sense of beauty and belonging. We felt honored and cared for. We felt cherished.

I'm reminded of another dinner party, retold for us in Mark 14, where a woman poured out her costly perfume upon Jesus' head. Others grew huffy at such wasted extravagance, murmuring that she should have sold the expensive oil and given her earnings to the poor. They scolded her for such carelessness.

But Jesus? He told them to leave her alone and praised her for this sacrifice of beauty:

> *She has done what she could; she has anointed my body beforehand for burial. (Mark 14:8)*

Do you see the importance of Jesus Christ's perspective?

She has done what she could. None of us can meet the needs of everyone, nor are we called to. But it is too easy to become frozen, paralyzed by the urgent necessities of others. We feel discouraged because we cannot possibly do everything that we want to for the people around us; we are not able to love as we feel that we ought.

This passage in Mark serves to offer a helpful path for each one of us. Look around at what you already possess, and use it to bless another, sacrificially giving in small, beautiful measures to the glory of God. Just do what you can. Others might not notice our efforts, but Jesus does, and he gladly affirms them. We are proving our faithfulness to him as we love in dear ways. In love he sacrificed for us; in love for him we sacrifice for others.

Pause and study the landscape of your ordinary life through an eternal perspective, asking the Holy Spirit to infuse you with holy love.

We can each love in some way, doing what we can, giving what we have.

<hr/>

That scorching summer day, Joel's father was facing the reality of another round of painful surgery for his dear son. He could have slumped inward, staying tucked away in their hotel room, feeling sorry for himself.

I am grateful he did not. Facing the relentless, gaping crowds, he proudly carried his only son toward the fray, searching out an ice-cream stand while inviting us into natural conversation.

I witnessed the age-old love of God that day, as Joel ate his ice cream, bit by bit, aided by a loving father who gave and gave and gave some more. May we do likewise.

God might not orchestrate our personal circumstances to include a traumatic injury. Perhaps he is calling you to slender opportunities to love others well, such as buying an extra box of granola bars, and handing them out to homeless people on your way to work. Or sacrificing a few hours each week to serve in the church nursery, loving children by teaching them about Jesus, even though you do not really want to. Or maybe he is prompting you to awaken a little earlier each morning to pray for your family, your neighbors, and your church. You will forfeit sleep, or the late-night news the night before. Love gives sacrificially.

Genuine love always requires loss. Sacrificial love is just that—personal loss turned to another's gain. God sees and treasures such heartfelt sacrifice, however small it is in the world's eyes.

And may that be our highest aim—to please God, who modeled the greatest sacrifice from a place of love:

> *But God shows his love for us in that while we were still sinners, Christ died for us. (Romans 5:8)*

TWO

Joy: Holding onto Jesus

*"These things I have spoken to you, that my joy may
be in you, and that your joy may be full."
(John 15:11)*

I was at the grocery store the other day, exchanging pleasantries with the cashier while placing my items on the conveyor belt. As she rang up my purchases, a store manager jogged over, warning me to be careful as I returned to my car. A heated argument had erupted in the parking lot between two shoppers, and authorities had been notified.

"Why are people so angry these days?" The cashier sighed, shrugging at her own question before adding, "Is there any joy left in this world?"

I considered her words the entire way home.

After all, life can certainly feel pretty joyless sometimes. Yet as Christians, we hold the golden key to joy. The Holy

Spirit is at work within us, urging our sleepy hearts to remember that Jesus has given us every reason to sparkle with happy contentment.

Why? Christ has crushed our sins, smashing every single one, to bring us home to God. This is our freedom: Christ's life for ours. Through all of life's pain, we stand free—an undeserving yet holy people awaiting the beauty of heaven. The more we gaze on these realities, the more we will see joy growing in our hearts.

These thoughts took me back in time to my childhood days spent on Old Mill Road.

And at the center of those memories stands dear Mrs. Dawson.

The street of my childhood was a beautiful old New England country road, which threaded its way through field and farmland, culminating in a tiny cul-de-sac.

Our family lived at the top of this road in a quaint, whitewashed farmhouse. Although old, the dwelling had been neatly divided into four humble apartments and was beautifully maintained by our faithful landlord. I loved our modest home and the surrounding peaceful countryside. Every night, after baths and prayers, my brother and I pressed our small noses to the cold windowpane of our expansive bedroom window, surveying the inky, star-studded sky that soared high above the back field.

In unison, we recited our simple rhythm of closure—proffering our childish goodnights to the world before succumbing to dreamland.

"Goodnight God. Goodnight moon and stars. And goodnight to every single person in the whole wide world, except for David Dawson."

The Dawson family dwelt at the end of our road, their home tucked within a wooded lot. Curling behind their house was a railroad track.

David was the family's middle child, one of five. His two older siblings had long since graduated from high school, and David's younger brother and sister were elementary students and school chums of ours.

David, however, was a bully.

He picked fights with anyone and everyone, including his younger siblings, pushing neighborhood children off of bikes, stealing lunch money, and making life as miserable as possible for others.

My brother and I somehow managed to evade him while helplessly observing his disturbing behaviors. Eclipsing him from our goodnight ritual was the strongest nod to justice that we could muster.

In time, our mother struck up a friendship with Mrs. Dawson and was thereby invited for a visit at the Dawson residence.

So one bright afternoon my brother and I joined her, skipping down the road to meet Mrs. Dawson for the first time. I was nervous that David might have inherited his mean streak from his mother, but I was wrong. She was nothing like her lanky, mean-spirited child, but stood short and round, with wide, gentle eyes, and an enormous smile.

"Well hello, Kristin and Tommy! I am delighted to meet you!" She laughed, patting first my brother's shoulder and then mine. "Welcome! Won't you come in for some lemonade?"

We nodded and followed her indoors to the kitchen.

Her radiant smile landed upon me, warming me in a blanket of joy.

"Excuse the mess!" she laughed as she waved toward the stove and sink. "I have been cooking."

Pots and pans filled the sink and littered the stovetop, and a mouth-watering aroma of Italian meat sauce enveloped the room.

She chuckled good-naturedly. "There is always work to be done! A mother's work is never done, is it?"

My eyes took in this lovely woman, perched in her bright kitchen. She was different from other mothers, exuding joy rather than worry. I spotted a large wooden cross decorating the wall, with a small tin sign hanging next to it that read: *Jesus loves me, this I know.*

Such placards were uncommon in those days. I paid attention to those words, glowing like the afternoon sun which danced through the curtained window, matching this cheerful woman.

"Do you like the cross?" She tilted her head, studying my gaze.

I nodded.

She grinned. "Me too."

As we sipped our cold drinks she called out for her two youngest children, who came dashing from another room.

"Hello my loves. Please take Kristin and Tommy out to the zipline. Have some fun!"

Did we ever! The zipline was not too high above the ground and stretched from maple to pine to oak. We had the time of our lives, flying about the yard, windblown and breathless and energized by such superhero speed. Mrs. Dawson and my mother stepped outdoors to watch us, and Mrs. Dawson's joy in our simple pleasure radiated from her being. She clapped her hands as we zipped by, laughing and waving. The afternoon passed far too quickly and suddenly it was time to go home.

She slipped my brother and I an oatmeal cookie as we prepared to leave.

"Come back anytime, kiddos. Our house is your house!"

She grinned as she waved and we skipped down the driveway. I glanced back and watched her wrap her short arms around her youngest two, embracing them in a pleasant squeeze as her eyes closed in delight. It is an image I will never forget.

Mr. Dawson, in contrast, was the street's curmudgeon. He was kind exactly one time each year, playing Santa Claus on Christmas Eve to neighborhood children, hefting a large bag of wrapped gifts from house to house, jingling a thickly corded rope studded with enormous silver bells, and shouting: "Ho! Ho! Ho! Merry Christmas!"

But on every other day, he growled and fussed—so different from his wife. With a pipe clenched between his teeth, he complained about the weather, the neighborhood, politics, his children's antics—you name it. As much as Mrs. Dawson remained open-handed, arms flung wide, drawing people in, her husband was arms crossed, closed off, cynical.

Mrs. Dawson ignored his grumpiness, kissing his bearded cheek, and laughing at his bellyaching ways with a dismissive wave of her hand. While this certainly had a diminishing effect upon his perpetual negativity, it could not have been easy to live with such ongoing pessimism from a man who declined her repeated requests to accompany her to church.

Soon after our visit David began to stir up more serious trouble at school. Mrs. Dawson did all she could, enforcing strict disciplinary measures, and openly shared her sorrow with her friends. Yet I remember playing at their house during that time, marveling at how this woman could remain so upbeat with a grumpy husband and a troubled son.

Her joy was both different and contagious. The secret, as you may have guessed, was that her spiritual roots plunged deep. I heard her often speak about God as though he was standing in the room with us, real and alive, *which of course he was*. It was a new and unusual experience for me, and I longed for this same treasure.

She was a glowing candle in a darkened world, a lamplight fueled by this truth: "Jesus loves me, this I know." The cross and signpost in her kitchen were maps leading to Mrs. Dawson's demeanor, the impetus for such powerful joy. It was impossible to miss.

This honest-to-goodness joy?

It was wildly attractive.

<hr />

One day we visited their house again, this time greeted by two German Shepherd puppies, who were frolicking and wrestling on the front porch. Mrs. Dawson opened the screened door, dusting off her floured hands on her checkered apron—which draped nearly to her ankles, given her small stature.

"Hello!" she waved with an infectious laugh. "Want to meet the boys?"

She pointed to the two chunky pups. Their paws were enormous.

"You bought puppies!" I said, running to scratch their silky heads. They stretched lazily, yawning and closing their eyes while soaking up the attention.

I had pined for a dog my entire life, all seven years of it. I could have camped out on that front porch forever.

"Actually, Kristin, we didn't buy them," Mrs. Dawson explained. "Let me tell you the story.

"Last week I was washing dishes after dinner when I thought I heard a whining noise. I stepped outside but heard nothing more. A little later I heard it again, but when Mr. D. and I walked around our yard all was quiet.

"And then, in the middle of the night, while we were fast asleep, we heard piercing wails and barking. We grabbed our flashlights and crept around the backyard. The noise grew louder and louder as we approached the railroad tracks. That is when we saw it."

"Saw what?" My brother and I said in unison, our eyes widening.

"An old, tattered pillowcase, fastened tightly to the railroad tracks. The pillowcase was fluttering, and when we untied it, these two cuties were staring at us."

I gulped, tears threatening.

Mrs. Dawson patted my head.

"But isn't it wonderful that God let us find them? Someone wanted to kill them but we rescued them!"

She smiled, so softhearted, a tear slipping down her cheek. As she picked up one of the pups he rewarded her by licking her entire face.

She laughed again, her belly jiggling.

"It gives me so much joy to know that we saved them."

—

I eventually lost touch with Mrs. Dawson, as I grew up, got married, and moved far away. Yet to this day, when the word joy is mentioned, it is Mrs. Dawson's face that burns brightly in my memory.

I still envision that sunny kitchen, with pots and pans and papers scattered across the countertop. I remember the shortest of women who rose to the highest of heights in my mind, with kind eyes and a generous smile. And I think of her with those puppies she had saved—who would otherwise have been doomed to perish—as they licked her face in happy adoration, gratitude, affection.

Isn't that a picture of what happens in our hearts when God rescues us? He saved Mrs. Dawson, and she was joyfully infused with the Holy Spirit. She was just like her puppies, loving her Master with complete adoration, affection, and gratitude.

This is the dynamic that the apostle Paul captured in his letter to believers in Colossae. He prayed that they would be…

> … *strengthened with all power, according to his glorious might, for all endurance and patience with joy; giving thanks to the Father, who has qualified you to share in the inheritance of the saints in light.*

> *He has delivered us from the domain of darkness and*
> *transferred us to the kingdom of his beloved Son, in*
> *whom we have redemption, the forgiveness of sins.*
> *(Colossians 1:11-14)*

Before God's intercession, you and I were more helpless than those puppies tied to the train track: we were imprisoned in "the domain of darkness," and utterly unable to free ourselves. But God has reached down into our plight and "transferred us to the kingdom of his beloved Son"—a dramatic and majestic rescue that no power of hell can undo.

And here's something more that we sometimes forget: God did not rescue us reluctantly. It gave him joy to do it.

"The LORD your God is in your midst, a mighty one who will save," the prophet Zephaniah promised the people of Judah as they faced the prospect of exile. "He will rejoice over you with gladness; he will quiet you by his love; he will exult over you with loud singing" (Zephaniah 3:17). And now, this side of Jesus' death and resurrection, it's as though God looks at his people, and says, like Mrs. Dawson: *It gives me so much joy to know that I saved them.*

So it's to this joyful God that we run when our wells of joy run dry. We pray with Paul:

> *May the God of hope fill you with all joy and peace*
> *in believing, so that by the power of the Holy Spirit*
> *you may abound in hope. (Romans 15:13)*

Always looking to Jesus, our bright morning star.

It is striking that these joy-focused prayers emerged from the heart of a man who had been beaten, tortured, shipwrecked, and imprisoned for his faith in God.

Joy does not make sense apart from who we have become as Christ-followers. It is rather strange, isn't it—given the ongoing misery permeating our world? Joy contradicts our natural human senses.

Mr. Dawson's grumpiness actually made perfect sense. His life was dreadfully burdensome considering his terribly rebellious son, financial struggles, and ongoing health dilemmas. Of course he groaned and bellyached! Who wouldn't gripe?

The person being daily renewed. The one with a heart pulsing with a genuine understanding of Christ's work completed on their behalf.

Mrs. Dawson was met with matching obstacles to her husband's, but there remained a stark difference: her heart-perspective. The cross, where Jesus bled and hung and died, remained at the core of her soul. Such focus kindled a lifelong flame: *Jesus loves me, this I know.*

Healthy fruit grows from healthy branches which are strengthened by strong roots. If we are rooted in the cross, the Holy Spirit grows joy in our hearts. He energizes us with reminders of Jesus, bringing to mind the depths of the work our Savior accomplished when he died for us, and the heights of his love that this proves.

We are unable to "homebrew" joy. It is only a work of the Holy Spirit. But neither do we sit back and do absolutely nothing. Rather, we must earnestly seek to cultivate the kind of rich soil in our hearts which will foster the growth of such fruit. Time spent reading and meditating upon the Bible will grow our pleasure in Christ. Feasting on the preaching of God's word each week at church is another fertilizer for our soil. And we must refuse to make space for sulking, complaining, and self-pity to grow. Instead, let us remember to till the soil of our hearts with ongoing prayer, asking God to bless and fill us with his joy.

No matter your station in life—rich or poor, young or old, pastor or parishioner—if you are a Christian, the joy of the Lord is *yours*. A joy impervious to circumstances.

"Joy," the author Elisabeth Elliot once wrote, "is not the absence of suffering but the presence of God." David, in the Old Testament, knew this well. For a large part of his life he was despised by King Saul, who hunted him down with the intent to murder him. Despite such frightening hardships, he wrote psalms that testified to the source of his joy:

> *I bless the LORD who gives me counsel; in the night also my heart instructs me. I have set the LORD always before me; because he is at my right hand, I shall not be shaken. Therefore my heart is glad, and my whole being rejoices; my flesh also dwells secure. For you will not abandon my soul to Sheol or let your holy one see corruption. You make known to me the path of life; in your presence there is fullness of joy; at your right hand are pleasures forevermore.*
> *(Psalm 16:7–11)*

May we do the same, choosing to trust our Redeemer, remembering that *Jesus loves me, this I know*. He is with us and he will keep us; as his sheep we are favored beyond measure, and Christ will bring us home to God's right hand.

When the test comes back positive, and a long season of treatment lies ahead: *Jesus loves me, this I know*.

When your boss tells you he is sorry, but cuts must be made: *Jesus loves me, this I know*.

When your children make foolish decisions, and your heart is crushed: *Jesus loves me, this I know*.

When your To-Do list is growing longer and longer, and you are tired: *Jesus loves me, this I know*.

When this earthly life seems a puzzle, and the pieces do not fit together: *Jesus loves me, this I know*.

Christian, joy is *yours*.

Joy to the world, the Lord has come
Let earth receive her king!
Let every heart prepare him room
And heaven and nature sing
And heaven and nature sing
And heaven, and heaven and nature sing.
(Isaac Watts – 1719)

I am not asking whether you know things about
him but do you know God, are you enjoying God, is

God the center of your life, the soul of your being, the source of your greatest joy? He is meant to be.
(Martin Lloyd Jones)

THREE

Peace: The Calm in the Storm

*"You keep him in perfect peace whose mind is stayed
on you because he trusts in you."*
(Isaiah 26:3)

Have you ever stood at the edge of a stormfront as the winds begin to gust, soft rain turning to icy, pelting drops of heavy snow? What is your first impulse?

Perhaps, if you are like me, it is to dash to a place of comfort and safety. To seek shelter in the strength of a well-built structure, preferably home.

There is peace in physical safety, isn't there?

But what happens when the storms aren't weather related? What do we do when, amidst the normal rhythms of daily life, an unbidden situation flares, turning the mundane into a stormy disaster which seems anything but safe? How can we maintain a peace-filled heart when God permits a frightening medical diagnosis, crushing financial loss, an accident, trauma, or relational disaster to pass through his sovereign hands?

⸻

I descend from a long line of fearful women. Anxiety, you see, is the very opposite of peace. One of my sharpest childhood memories takes me back to the stuffy, over-heated apartment of my great-grandparents, observing Great-Grandmother as she rocked back and forth in her heirloom chair, peppering her daughter (my grand-mother) with worries like bullets from a rifle.

What if the money runs out? What if I slip in the tub? What if I die before your father? What if...? What if...? What if...?

Fear was the ever-nagging shadow, painting frown lines and forehead creases on nearly all of the female faces in our family tree. Growing up in this perpetual state of worry was the life that I knew. Fear was passively taught, not always in a gloom-and-doom way, but by perpetually living on the defensive—with a "glass half-empty" mindset. As a little girl I followed where my ancestors led, with a fear of getting lost, the fear of giants, and an overwhelming fear at the mere thought of being called upon in school.

Yet such fear stood at odds with what I heard when I entered our church sanctuary each Sunday.

My confusion grew while paying close attention to my Sunday school teacher, who spoke of a wise and judicious Jesus—God in flesh—who remained peaceful, even in the middle of petrifying storms. Jesus told his followers to "fear not." Even the wind and the waves obeyed him, ceasing all motion at his bidding!

So what was I to do, with a family dotted with worry-warts, who although fanning themselves next to me in church, spent the remainder of the week fretting about most everything?

One day, God whispered to me through the teaching of his word, beckoning me to choose peace over fear. What began as a normal week turned into anything but. A deadly storm was closing in, and no one, including meteorologists, realized it.

And in the middle of this blizzard?

My father went missing.

⟜

I was just shy of six when the storm of the century struck.

It was 1978, and my father had already left for work by the time I woke up. An elementary teacher with a 45-minute drive to work, his unfailing custom was to arrive hours before the students, grading papers and completing lesson plans blissfully undisturbed, in the stretch of those dark, early hours.

This particular morning began much like any other. Forecasters had called for light snow to begin in the later afternoon—a common state of affairs during long, New England winters. I pulled on my warm socks, ate my oatmeal, and climbed onto the school bus for my half-day of kindergarten. I would be home long before the snow began, and in time for a grilled cheese-and-soup lunch with my mother and younger brother.

But the snow started early, confusing all meteorologists. By the time I entered my classroom it had begun descending in earnest and was rapidly accumulating at what quickly became an alarming rate. Our school superintendent, with one eye on his watch and the other upon the swirling, snow-filled skies, sighed and signaled for all buses to return, a mere 90 minutes after dropping students off.

Those were different days, and parents were not even notified that their children were being sent home early. My mother was stunned when I knocked on our front door—stunned *and* frightened. She peeked out the window at the snowy skies from our top floor apartment situated within an old farmhouse. My early arrival home, the torrential snow, plus the whipping wind gusts had her unsettled.

Those worry lines between her young brows ran like canyons, and she seemed to fade far away from my brother and me.

"What's wrong?" I tugged at her sweater. Snow had never been a worry before.

"Go play with your brother, Kristin." Her hand was on our kitchen's rotary phone.

My brother dragged out his box of blocks from beneath his bed, and we began to build roadways, filling up the narrow dining-room floor with elaborate paths for his toy cars.

I heard our mother dial.

"Hello—Charlie! What time did he leave? Good! Yes, I know. Never seen it fall so fast. Thank you." She hung up. The worry between her eyebrows diminished, and I felt my stomach calm. Charlie was my father's boss.

"Kids, we are in for a Northeaster! Your dad's school closed early and he should be home any time now." Her voice was back to normal as she filled the tea kettle with tap water and set it to boil, and then rooted about in the cupboard for the Swiss Miss.

"Who wants marshmallows?"

"Meee!" My brother and I sang in unison.

Steaming tomato soup and grilled cheese sandwiches came and went. Lunchtime was long since over, and my father was still not home. Our mother paced between our prominent living-room windows, tall panes that provided an exquisite view of our tree-lined yard, street, and pond, now iced over and snowy white.

Her back-and-forth movements stopped only as she paused to call her sister and her mother. The words tumbled out in hushed sobs:

"It's falling fast… drifts impossibly high… trapped… state of emergency… might never come home."

The anxiety festered and multiplied like a virus, becoming a scratchy, uncomfortable blanket which suffocated our little apartment. Such a heavy presence, and I remember slipping into my bedroom, trying to escape the fear, tears threatening. There was no running away from this predicament. My dad was supposed to be home and he wasn't and the snow and ice were everywhere and only increasing.

I perched on my bed and remembered my Sunday school teacher.

A short, stocky man with shocking blue eyes and a mountain of black, unruly hair—plus a beard to match.

He reminded me of something. Yes—a hobbit!

"God," he had boomed not many Sundays before, "is in charge of the weather. In fact, he is in charge of every single thing. He makes good things and allows bad things which he turns into good things. And that is why we may have peace. Because we can always trust him."

"What's peace?" A boy in the front row asked, swinging his legs, and neglecting to raise his hand.

"Raise your hand, Jeffrey." Our teacher paused. "Peace is a hushed heart. Peace is when you trust God to be good no matter what happens. He is always good. Peace comes when you stop trying to squirm out of everything that is sad or hard. You sit still and believe in God."

He studied our small, upturned faces.

"Remember our song? About the wise man who built his house upon the rock? The house stood firm in the storm! But without trusting in God, you will be like the foolish man who built his house on the sand, and when the storms came the house went splat."

He clapped his thick hands and we jumped.

Pulling his readers from his shirt pocket, he picked up his Bible, and comfortably flipped through the fluttering, worn pages.

"Listen to what God says, children," and then he read from Matthew 7:24-27:

> *Everyone then who hears these words of mine and does them will be like a wise man who built his house on the rock. And the rain fell, and the floods came, and the winds blew and beat on that house, but it did not fall, because it had been founded on the rock. And everyone who hears these words of mine*

*and does not do them will be like a foolish man who
built his house on the sand. And the rain fell, and the
floods came, and the winds blew and beat against
that house, and it fell, and great was the fall of it.*

He removed his glasses and his eyes pierced ours.

"This kind of life will grow peace right here," he said as
he patted his heart softly. "And guess what? No one can
steal it."

His smile was radiant.

With these thoughts tumbling in my mind, I peeked
out my bedroom window to a whitewashed world. Our
backyard seemed to have disappeared altogether. The
drifts were climbing ever higher, filling me with an odd
sensation that our house had shrunk.

My father was out there! Somewhere.

I prayed on the inside: "Dear God, help me not to
worry. Keep Dad safe."

Running back to the living room, I placed my fingertips
on the icy window panes, hoping God would grant me
speedy evidence of my father's safety.

Nothing. Nothing at all but a thick white blanket
masking the yard, the trees, the pond, and the road.

Where was my father?

The clock ticked, hands creeping, daylight now receding.
By the time the dinner hour arrived and all was dark,

my brother and I had exhausted our puzzles and board games: *Parcheesi*, *Go Fish*, and *Old Maid*. Our mother had phoned my father's school again, in the hopes that he had turned back to seek shelter, but there was no answer. She phoned the police and received a busy signal every single time. Any shred of hope seemed to evaporate—and there was certainly no sign of dinner.

I studied my mother as I colored my workbooks, my prayer a quiet song. I remembered Jesus and his "Fear Nots," and the wise man's house built on the rock.

This was my first taste of genuine peace. It warmed me from the inside, calming my nervous stomach. My heart paused, steady and trusting God in tranquility.

God would make good things come from this scary day.

Mom switched on our ancient TV, which took a bit of time to warm up. There stood a news reporter, bundled in a heavy fur-lined coat with an enormous hood enveloping his face. He was hovering in a deep snowbank along Route 128, the road my father traveled every weekday. The wind was fierce, and he swayed.

"There have been multiple pileups, accidents, and now dozens of abandoned cars speckle the highway as the snow reaches as high as the car windows. People will likely be found frozen to death," he said.

The wind agreed, whipping noisily through his microphone as he squinted uncomfortably.

I sat perfectly still, my crayon in hand.

Our mother let out a sharp cry and turned the television off.

"What am I going to do…? Two children to raise… Where is he?" Her words felt wild, desperate, untethered to anything as her hands clutched the sides of her head and her pacing resumed.

"Mommy, where's Daddy?" said my little brother, his voice small.

"I don't know," she wailed, and began sobbing.

I saw my brother's lip begin to quiver, so I grabbed his hand and led him to the kitchen. I climbed a chair and pulled the Cheerios from the cupboard, pouring two small bowls, baptizing each with a drizzle of honey and a splash of milk.

Dinner.

The phone lines stopped working, and our lights flickered. My brother and I had brushed our teeth and changed into our footed pajamas when the front door blew open.

There stood our father, frozen stiff, eyebrows and eyelashes white, teeth chattering.

"I can't feel my hands or feet," he said with difficulty.

My mother was suddenly hugging him and wailing as my brother and I jumped up and down.

"I thought you were dead in a snowbank," she kept repeating.

My heart thudded, as I squeezed my own hands in delight. God had heard me!

Soon with a steaming cup of tea to warm his insides and a thick bathrobe plus layers of blankets added for good measure, my father sat in the living room and told us the story.

Upon an early school dismissal, he had packed up his briefcase and walked to the parking lot, scraping the snow and ice off of the windshield as his car warmed up. The driving was slow and dangerous, having blown in on the winds of surprise, catching road workers off guard. They simply could not keep pace as they attempted to clear roads by way of snowplow.

By the time our father had entered route 128, it was a virtual whiteout, and multiple cars had crashed into each other. The conditions were black-ice slippery with frightfully poor visibility. Other vehicles had broken down, engines quitting in such frigid and gusty conditions. My father's car eventually stopped, the engine huffing and puffing and conking out.

He did not know what to do. If he stayed inside the car, he would likely freeze to death. If he took his chances walking for help, he might be struck by a driver who could not see more than two feet ahead.

Nearly paralyzed by such a decision, his mind raced back and forth. He finally stepped out of the car, figuring his chances of being rescued would be greater outdoors. Walking, no matter how difficult, would at least keep his blood circulating. Thus, he set out.

After several minutes, he detected headlights behind him, as a car passed slowly, before stopping several yards ahead.

The red brake lights glowed through the falling snow.

"I have been rescued!" he thought with intoxicating relief, shuffling quickly to the car, the mere thought of warmth a deep consolation. He flung open the car's back door and crawled into the backseat, slamming the door closed while warming his cupped frozen hands by blowing on them.

Two stunned motorists, a middle-aged husband and wife, turned, gaping at this tall, snowy stranger now huddled in their backseat.

"What are you doing?" the man frowned.

"Oh! I thought you had stopped to help me!"

"No," he said. "We pulled over because we could scarcely see in front of us. My eyes needed a rest."

As it happened, they took pity on my father, and given the dire state of emergency, were kind enough to keep driving, albeit at a snail's pace, eventually dropping him at the top of our road: a road that descended by way of a long, winding path to our front door.

They had saved his life.

It was a miracle, truly. What should have taken 45 minutes on any given day took over eight hours. My father's journey from the top of our road to our front door in itself proved tedious and treacherous, with biting winds, ice, and mountains of snow.

As we later learned, people and pets vanished and then perished in those drifts, which eventually exceeded 15 feet.

I held God's peace inside my heart, warm and tender and different. I never spoke of that day, shy about the mystery that the God of all creation would hear me.

He had answered my prayers for my dad to come home, yet it was something more. He had filled me up with a calm that stopped my feet from pacing. I had given Jesus my heart only months before the Great Blizzard, and my roots were only small and tender.

This lovely fruit of peace was as tiny as a grape. It would take time and watering to grow deep roots. But it was a start.

Many view fear as an inevitability—as though we cannot help do anything *but* worry. Yet God's word repeatedly admonishes us *not* to worry. Rather than be crushed by this command, it can, instead, give us hope: there is, in fact, a different way to live. Peace is possible— even for you.

But let's be clear what God's call to peace *doesn't* mean. To embrace peace amidst fear is not to disregard our feelings. God designed us as emotional beings. We laugh, weep, mourn, and celebrate. Standing cold and stoic in the midst of horrific pain or tragedy is not what God asks of his children. We are frail beings stitched together by flesh and bone, fashioned from dust and rib. God sees our lowly state and loves us still: "The LORD shows compassion on those who fear him. For he knows our frame; he remembers that we are dust" (Psalm 103:13-14). He knows that even though we are made in his likeness, we are not *him*.

But neither are we to crawl through trials, chained to our emotions, allowing ourselves to be led by fickle feelings. Sometimes our unchecked worries will masquerade as positive taskmasters. Running through countless "what if" scenarios in our minds gives us *something* to do, offering us a sense of control. Oddly enough, worry often *feels* productive. But if left unchecked, fear becomes its own storm. Oftentimes it's not our actual circumstances that hold us captive, but imagined ones, robbing us of peace.

As Christians—infused with the Holy Spirit upon the moment of our regeneration—we can cling instead to the peace offered by Jesus, the solid rock beneath our feet in storms of distress. His words are true. When we build our lives upon them, we will stand firm on the day of judgment—like a house with solid foundations (Matthew 7:24-27). That being so, we can trust him to sustain us through anything that may happen in the interim. Just moments before his famous parable of the wise and foolish builders, in the Sermon on the Mount, Jesus assured his worry-prone listeners: *Your heavenly Father knows what you need.* "But seek first the kingdom of God and his righteousness, and all these things will be added to you" (6:32-33).

Peace is a gift from the Holy Spirit, who does not force himself upon us, but gently leads us to trust God and grow more like Jesus, little by little, day by day, as we learn to trust him first with one thing, and then another. Our sanctification in this area may well be gradual—but in the Spirit's power, it can certainly be real. How so? Because Christ himself, our Redeemer, was strung, bloody and marred, and then crucified on a cross. This cruel instrument of torture was thus transformed into the greatest instrument of peace.

Such truths are meant to soften and warm our hearts as we run to the arms of Jesus, turning over our cares and anxieties to him. We can know with certainty that he is with us, guiding our steps and holding us securely in his arms through the whipping winds and pelting rains. We are not asked to ignore our fears but to place them under the lordship of Christ, who has rescued us for eternity. This truth will serve to anchor us in any storm. Christ is our peace, our calm through all storms.

Perhaps you are thinking: "Easy for you to say! Your story ended happily." Yes, this particular story of mine did. My father came home. But peace is not bound to the perceived goodness of our desired outcomes. Peace is God's gift of calm through any storm, through any darkness. That doesn't make the darkness any less dark, or painful things any less painful. And yet in the midst of it, peace is the inner calm and the readiness to trust God, no matter what.

God knows the future and all of it has been sifted through his perfect hands. What a relief.

Sometimes the very way God grows the fruit of peace in our lives is by taking us, shaking, through the worst of storms.

A friend of mine was preparing dinner one evening many years ago, chopping vegetables for stir-fry, as her children played in the backyard. Her husband walked through the front door, loosening his tie after a long day's work.

He meandered to the kitchen island, just like every other ordinary evening, watching her as she guided the raw vegetables down the wooden board into the olive oil sizzling in the wok. She greeted him with "Hello, dear!" and he told her that he was leaving.

"Excuse me?" she laughed, thinking she heard incorrectly.

With no warning, no tears, no fanfare, and in a tone void of any emotion he said, "I have met someone else."

She was immobilized and in an utter state of shock as he packed a suitcase. She had not previously discerned so much as a whiff of trouble. He had been living a double life for quite some time, and she had been fooled.

Later—months later—she told me that as she wept for days afterward, her eyes swollen and puffy and mottled red, God had kindly graced her with his gentle peace. As she attempted to explain it to me, her eyes once more brimming with tears, she radiated a holy calm. I was stunned by her words, trying to imagine myself in her position. Here was a woman who was sitting hushed and shattered and still at the Lord's feet, clutching his robes as the storm raged relentlessly. With no assurance of any desirable outcome, and with her precious children crumbling in despair, her soul was at peace.

"I am still praying that he will turn back to God," she said in reference to the same man who had abandoned her, "and that we may reconcile and share our hard story as a testimony of hope for others." She paused, closed her eyes, and opened her outstretched hands, gently, palms raised. "But if God chooses to do something else, I will trust him still."

The Holy Spirit was close, and I felt his power, a rustling wind, beckoning me to consider this peace. "Help me to become like this, Lord," I prayed in my heart.

True peace is rare—and it shimmers, glowing soft and radiant in the life of its inhabitant. My friend had taken up residence in the lighthouse of the Lord, warm and safe and sorrowful as she sheltered high on the rock during the pounding storm as the lighthouse cast a bright spotlight to other ships at sea.

Her hopes of reconciliation never materialized. Her storm raged for years, ultimately crushing her earthly dreams to a heap of rubble. Her husband gave up on counseling. He never returned to her or the kids. As her children got older they wandered from God and church, suffering and confused.

Yet when, years later, we catch up again, I am once more struck by her demeanor. She smiles now, as she looks out the window, recounting her crisis season.

"I journaled letters to God every day during that time, and I have saved every notebook." She turns to me.

"Would you think it odd that I sometimes miss those days?" She plays with her shining wedding band, still new. Her story has come good, in some ways. And yet...

She glances out the window, sailing back to a private place. Wistful, almost.

The grandfather clock ticks in the hall.

"Those months after he left me... my heart was shredded, unmendable, but God stayed closer than ever, holding me." Her hand covers her heart as she closes her eyes and remembers. "Such intimacy with my heavenly Father. God is so, so good."

She opens her eyes and says softly, "I will never again fear the storms. He is my peace."

FOUR

Patience: The Secret Ingredient

"... with all humility and gentleness, with patience,
bearing with one another in love..."
(Ephesians 4:2)

I have a little theory and it goes like this: a true measure of one's patience is revealed behind the steering wheel.

I do not mean while one is cruising to the grocery store to pick up a gallon of milk on an average day with zero traffic. I mean while one is driving behind the slowest moving car, traveling far below the speed limit, when passing is not permitted, or while maneuvering the wheel in bumper-to-bumper traffic during rush hour.

We all experience bad days, but examine someone's driving over the course of days, weeks, and months, and it isn't so hard to detect patience, or lack thereof.

Mrs. Thatcher was a terrifying driver. As a grade-schooler, I played with her daughter regularly, and this mother of many flew along back roads in an old van, a vehicle which felt like an enormous box. I dreaded buckling up under her supervision and concocted ways to evade such experiences.

Please, Dad, can you pick me up at Kim's house on your way home from work? Please?

My pleadings worked on occasion, but not always.

I was prone to car sickness, which proved difficult as Mrs. Thatcher careened over potholes and curvy back roads, her foot accelerating at those moments when it would have been prudent to brake. She drove far over the speed limit, passing slow drivers as I clutched the door. Her daughter asked if I was alright.

"She's going too fast," I whispered, and Kim shrugged her shoulders and grinned.

"She does everything fast," Kim said.

She was right.

Mrs. Thatcher, whom you might imagine to be reckless in other areas of life, was anything but. A shiny gold bell sat perched upon a shelf on their kitchen wall. Dinner was served at precisely six o'clock, and when Mrs. Thatcher rang that tiny bell, everyone in the family had precisely two minutes to appear and be properly seated at the long table, hands washed. Tardiness resulted in being exiled to one's bedroom without sustenance. Period. No exceptions.

A list of chores was posted on the refrigerator, a detailed chart with color-coded tasks to be completed efficiently each day. Saturday mornings were set aside for deep cleaning projects: moving and dusting furniture, raking leaves, waxing floors, or tidying the garage. Little was left to chance.

One cold December afternoon, I was invited over to bake fancy Christmas cookies—a secret recipe passed down through many generations of the Thatcher family. Kim and I were fifth graders and terribly eager to bake independently. We were also thrilled to finally be on Christmas vacation. The Thatcher's Christmas tree stood tall and twinkly in front of the family-room window as soft snow fell from gray skies, pulling us into a jolly holiday spirit. Festive candy-cane aprons cinched our waists and hung long, nearly ankle-length. We plucked sticks of butter and speckled brown eggs from the refrigerator shelves and retrieved flour, baking soda, and salt from the pantry.

As we dumped the ingredients into the Thatcher's old, heavy-duty mixer, we erupted in laughter. Puffs of flour had poofed onto our faces, the speed of the mixer set too high beneath our unskilled hands.

"We're snowmen!" I giggled.

Kim took a spoonful of flour and tossed it in our faces, making them whiter.

Mrs. Thatcher motioned frantically toward us, grabbing our attention as she carried on a telephone conversation, the cord stretching across their kitchen.

"Don't waste flour," she mouthed, eyebrows furrowed.

Kim nodded and slowed the mixer speed. We wiped off the counter and our faces and quickly swept the floor as the oven preheated. I was relieved when her mother turned her attention back to her phone call.

"We forgot the almond extract!" Kim whispered to me moments before we were about to stuff the dough into the cookie press. "It's the most important secret ingredient!"

She pulled the step stool from the pantry closet and climbed up, stretching for the highest cupboard. She returned with a large bottle in hand and removed the lid.

"Here is the magic ingredient, Master Chef," she said with a faux British accent, taking a bow and handing me the extract.

We giggled and I copied her, taking an even lower bow than she. "No, you are Master Chef!" I answered, offering back the bottle.

In the handoff the bottle slipped and fell against the counter, the contents glugging down the cabinets and pooling onto the linoleum floor.

We were in trouble now.

"Girls!" Mrs. Thatcher's voice was shrill. "Such silliness! What a waste! Do you know how expensive almond extract is? I cannot believe you two."

Kim offered to clean it up, grabbing a dishcloth. My cheeks burned as I nodded in agreement, apologizing while not knowing what to do next. Mrs. Thatcher wanted no help.

"Ahhhh! So frustrating! Go to your room and wait for Kristin's mother to pick her up."

I felt awful. Foolish. We had not meant any harm in our silliness, but Kim's mom had a quick temper.

To be fair, I *had* witnessed this woman do many kind things for others at school and likewise at church—charitable acts of generosity and kindness. But those were always done on *her* timetable. This woman clearly did not suffer fools, and it seemed as though nearly everyone, at least in her opinion, landed in that camp—from other motorists in her way, to tardy dinner arrivals, to over-excited fifth-grade bakers. Her impatience often flared, and to the detriment of others.

One wrong move or perceived grievance and she hit the roof, just as her foot hit the gas pedal.

~~~

Months later, my Girl Scout troop gathered to work on earning our cooking badge. My friend Rachel's mother, Mrs. Gould, offered their kitchen to the group, also volunteering to instruct us in the fine art of cake-baking.

I was given a ride to the residence by Mrs. Gould herself. She asked the young ladies in her vehicle to buckle up, speaking kindly, and smiling knowingly in the rearview mirror as we giggled and chatted as is the tendency of ten-year-old girls.

She was gracious and unhurried in her driving, gently waving another driver ahead at a four-way stop. And those curvy New England roads? They melted softly beneath us as she obeyed the speed limit, maneuvering the wheel calmly, taking the curves with utmost care. I did not feel carsick at all.

~~~

All the same, once in the kitchen I was gun-shy, given the recent spilled-extract-episode, so I hung back against the wall, allowing the other girls the opportunity to measure and stir. I did not want to make a mistake and embarrass myself all over again.

"Angel food cake requires egg whites, and plenty of them, girls," Mrs. Gould smiled at each of us as we gathered around for instructions. "And there must not be a speck of yolk or shell in the whites. If there is, the eggs won't beat into soft peaks. And soft peaks are necessary for our cake."

Sunlight streamed into her pretty yellow kitchen.

"Let's begin with me showing you how to separate the yolk from the egg."

She cracked the brown egg against the bowl, holding two half-shells in either hand.

"I will move the yolk back and forth, from shell to shell, and allow the whites to drain into the bowl beneath my hands."

"Voilà!" She laughed as she worked. "Now girls, it's your turn to try."

The next half hour was spent practicing, one at a time. None of us experienced fast success.

Tears stung my eyes when I stepped toward the little island as everyone watched, cracking first one egg, then two, then three and four, leaving fragments of shell scattered in the bowl, and a swirl of yolks in the whites.

"There, there, it's ok! Not to worry, Kristin. These things take practice." She took my hand. "Come with me, dearie. I want to show you something."

Together we walked to their refrigerator, and Mrs. Gould opened the door. "Look what I bought!"

Before me was a shelf with at least ten cartons of eggs.

Her eyes crinkled. "We have all afternoon and plenty

of eggs to use for practice. Don't worry! Practice makes perfect, and practice takes time!"

She smiled at each face in her kitchen.

"A good baker must be patient. And patience takes time to grow. Always remember this."

Our angel food cake baked tall and lovely and golden brown that afternoon. Mrs. Gould offered us iced lemonade with a sprig of mint in cobalt goblets, which we sipped gracefully, feeling quite grown up and especially fancy. Once the cake had cooled, she sliced it and added a spoonful of strawberries and a dollop of whipped cream for good measure.

I had never tasted a finer dessert.

It has been 40 years since I stood in that bright kitchen, where patience was the soft, exquisite background music, allowing me to exhale and to keep trying.

Proverbs 31:25 describes the "excellent wife" like this: "Strength and dignity are her clothing, and she laughs at the days to come."

While strength and dignity were certainly the fabric of Mrs. Gould's clothing, that was not all she wore. It was her soft cloak of patience that wrapped up the essence of her personhood, warming the hearts of everyone.

Not once have I cracked an egg or separated yolks from their whites without remembering the patience of that dear woman.

~

The spiritual fruit of patience, like other qualities, is usually slow to grow and ripen. God often teaches us patience through seasons of inconvenient circumstances, spent with deeply frustrating people. In such seasons, we always have a choice: to either patiently cooperate with the Holy Spirit through obedience to God, or to grieve the Holy Spirit through impatience.

One blossoms into a fruit of calm acceptance, while the second shows up in restless agitation, shrouded in a dark cloud of frustration.

And while patience serves to honor God and bless others, impatience stings and tears down anyone in its path—a rotten fruit displeasing to the Lord.

A most striking biblical portrait of patience is found in Jacob in Genesis 29. Up to this point, Jacob is not portrayed as a particularly likable character—we see him withhold a small kindness from his brother, and then gravely deceive his father.

When Jacob meets Rachel, he falls deeply in love with this beauty. He asks her father's permission to marry her, and Laban agrees.

But first? Jacob is required to work for seven long years for his bride, and the Bible tells us that the days seemed like nothing, because his love for her was so great (Genesis 29:20).

Finally, the marriage ceremony takes place, his veiled bride by his side, but when morning breaks, Jacob is shocked to see that he has been tricked by Laban into marrying Rachel's older and less attractive sister, Leah.

Jacob challenges Laban, but is persuaded to complete the obligatory week-long marital festivities before being allowed to marry his beloved Rachel. This second union comes with yet another steep price tag: the promise to work another seven long years—all because of Laban's deception.

Jacob's work in obtaining his bride is a portrait of long-suffering. He worked many years for Rachel because he loved her. This is a likeness of Christ, isn't it? He is our bridegroom, who patiently suffered the terrors of crucifixion to win his bride, the true church (Ephesians 5:25-27).

In contrast, the Bible paints a portrait of *impatience* in the life of Jacob's grandparents, Sarai and Abram. God had promised Abram that his descendants would be as numerous as the stars in the sky (Genesis 15:5). But Sarai, Abram's wife, grows tired of waiting years and years for God's promise to be fulfilled. She and her husband are in their old age, with no offspring, long past their child-bearing years, and living in tents. From Sarai's vantage point, nothing is happening to indicate that God will fulfill his pledge.

Sarai has had enough of waiting. Never mind what God had promised—she decides that it is time to take matters firmly into her own hands.

In her impatience, Sarai cooks up a plan, convincing her husband to take Sarai's servant-woman, an Egyptian named Hagar, into his quarters, so as to speed things up in the baby-and-future-heir-department (Genesis 16). The baby that Hagar conceives through Abram will become the property of Sarai.

Once Hagar is pregnant, she despises this woman who would soon take possession of her little one—a baby boy born nine months later named Ishmael. And why wouldn't she despise Sarai? Hagar had been used by both Abraham and Sarai—a means to their end. A horrible and selfish decision birthed from impatience, willfully disregarding the Lord's promise and refusing to accept his timetable.

And aren't there always casualties conceived from our exasperation and restlessness—our stubborn unwillingness to wait upon the Lord causing suffering for others?

Unlike Sarai and Abram, God is perfectly patient. Our heavenly Father is unrushed in his plans. Despite the impatience of Sarai and Abram, God keeps his promise. In the very next chapter he renames this couple Abraham and Sarah—"Abraham" meaning "Father of many." In time he allows Sarah, at the ripe old age of 90, to conceive and give birth to Isaac, who becomes the father of Jacob, who in turn fathers the twelve tribes of Israel, leading, generations later, to the arrival of the promised Messiah, our Savior Jesus Christ.

Yes, God is patient.

Perhaps at times you believe that you are on the final egg in life: bits of shell are floating pathetically in the bowl, and the yolk and the white have collided, ruining the cake batter. Worse still, your impatience has flared and you are certain that God's refrigerator stands empty. Three strikes, and you are out.

Nonsense! God has no shortage of eggs, and he stands patiently, arms outstretched, giving you another opportunity. Rejoice when convicted of your own impatience! Such conviction is a prompting of the Holy Spirit to lead you to repentance, and you may revel in the providential opportunity to run back to our patient heavenly Father.

> *The Lord is not slow to fulfill his promise as some count slowness, but is patient toward you, not wishing that any should perish, but that all should reach repentance. (2 Peter 3:9)*

And Jesus promises us:

> *All that the Father gives me will come to me, and whoever comes to me I will never cast out.*
>
> *(John 6:37)*

We see clearly from these verses that God is patient and that his refrigerator remains infinitely full; he will never turn away a soul who truly seeks him. He does not desire for any one of his sheep to perish. So go ahead and joyfully run back to him.

Think of it like this: Why did God send Jesus? To atone for one sin? Two sins?

Three strikes and you are out?

Never. God sent his Son to bear the sins of the world. In his perfect patience, God provided a path for his children to return to him.

That path is faith in Jesus.

May we revel in our Creator's generous gift of patience, and in turn, practice such patience toward others.

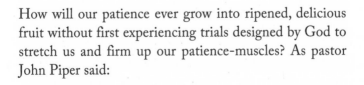

How will our patience ever grow into ripened, delicious fruit without first experiencing trials designed by God to stretch us and firm up our patience-muscles? As pastor John Piper said:

Every day, in every circumstance, God is always doing 10,000 things in your life, but you might be aware of only three of them. (https://www. desiringgod.org/articles/god-is-always-doing-10000-things-in-your-life)

Yes, God is working in a myriad of ways, and although our hardships often feel quite isolated, when strung together they mold and shape us into a fragrant bouquet of patience—if only we choose to press into God, waiting patiently upon him.

The truth? It is highly unlikely that we will face the precise tests of the Old Testament patriarchs like Jacob and Abraham—duped into marrying the sibling of our intended spouse or anticipating the birth of a child at the ripe old age of 90. But we *will* be presented with a myriad of other frustrating situations.

Perhaps the seemingly small habits of your spouse are driving you mad—he leaves those dirty dishes in the sink or promises to take out the trash but never does. She spends more time looking at her phone than asking about your day, or forgets to schedule an oil change, again. Maybe your child leaves their laundry scattered on the floor, or whines when reminded to finish their homework. Then there is that nosy coworker who pesters you, refusing to leave you to work in peace.

Or perhaps you are simply stuck in daily rush-hour traffic, moving behind slow or incompetent drivers.

Maybe there are deeper issues: you are being gossiped about repeatedly, unfairly misrepresented, or continually mocked for your faith. You have had it up to here, and are impatient that nothing is changing for the better.

What shall we do, when presented with these daily opportunities to lean one way (patience) or the other (impatience) in our responses? Does it even matter?

It most certainly does.

The author Jerry Bridges wrote the following:

> *Every day God patiently bears with us, and every day we are tempted to become impatient with our friends, neighbors, and loved ones. And our faults and failures before God are so much more serious than the petty actions of others that tend to irritate us! God calls us to graciously bear with the weaknesses of others, tolerating them and forgiving them even as he has forgiven us. ("The Practice of Godliness," NavPress, 2016, p 174)*

The question therefore becomes this: Will we trust God and walk through moments of frustration as a person of patience, reveling in obedience to the Holy Spirit who abides within our believing souls? Or will we take matters into our own hands, impatient and exasperated in the depths of our spirits?

I remember Mrs. Gould, and consider her patient kindness, so like the Spirit of God toward us. May we each take someone to the proverbial refrigerator, with a "Come here, dearie," showing off the dozens of treasured eggs at our disposal—supplied by God himself; our unhurried patience shining brightly in the sparkling, sunny kitchen of our souls.

And then I consider Mrs. Thatcher, impatient and hurried and a slave to her own timetable. These behaviors inevitably hurt others and are unlike our patient, heavenly

Father. When your patience feels stretched thin and you snap like Mrs. Thatcher, remember this: God is waiting patiently, eager to forgive all of his children who approach him with a contrite heart. Such repentance is proof of the fresh and mighty breeze of the Holy Spirit, sweeping clean our hearts through the power of God's forgiveness.

Yes, God is mercifully patient even as we are impatient.

Be encouraged, Christian, as you pray to grow stronger roots, bearing fruit in patience. Face each annoyance, each trial as it appears, moment-by-moment, and day-by-day. Ask yourself, "How may I be more patient in this present time? How may I yield to the kindness of the Holy Spirit residing within my soul?"

The Holy Spirit will comfort and help you. Patience is enchanting, drawing others in. A welcoming fruit born of God.

The secret ingredient in the Christian's life.

FIVE

Kindness: A Place of Refuge

*"The native people showed us unusual kindness, for
they kindled a fire and welcomed us all, because it
had begun to rain and was cold."*
(Acts 28:2)

She served my daughter and I coffee on a tray, walking
carefully up the stairs to our guest bedroom—eyes
glowing and face radiant on a dark and chilly morning.
The mugs sat heavy, sturdy and smooth, surrounded
by a small pitcher of half-and-half milk, glittery sugar
cubes, and stevia sweetener. As she placed the tray carefully upon the dresser, I noticed her fuzzy slippers, cozy
and warm.

Meet Jill, who is unusually kind.

Our paths first crossed when we discovered each other's writing online, and we were kindred spirits from the start. The two of us hold much in common: mothers to four (three sons and one daughter each), married to husbands with the same first name (Jon), voracious readers, utterly captivated by Jan Karon's *Mitford* books and enchanted by the delight of *words*. And as devoted Christ-followers? Our deepest thirst is for God and his word.

Jill reached out and introduced herself through email, and correspondence sailed between us, crossing time zones and closing our 1200-mile gap.

One ordinary day she messaged me, inviting me to attend a Christian conference with her: "Oh! And also? I would love for you to stay in our home!"

To which I responded, "Yes!"

Never mind that we had not even spoken, only emailed. My daughter, Lauren, and I grabbed a hold of this unexpected opportunity, embracing adventure together, and spinning the invite into a road trip. Time was fleeting and I knew it—in a few short months my favorite girl's college adventure would begin, and the door would close to impromptu mother-daughter trips.

God was kind to orchestrate this unexpected journey in the middle of a taxing season. Our family had been trudging through what felt like an endless bog of molasses: month upon month of disturbing heartache—a season clouded by sorrow and spiritual warfare darker and deeper than anything we had previously faced. In fact, it felt as though this path might never be clear. The journey was both messy and exhausting.

But God, who is more kind than all others, had for us ordained an unexpected place of refuge; a reprieve. I only wish that my husband could have joined us, but the spiritual oppression was raging within our church, and he is the senior pastor. While this was not the time for him to take a trip, he encouraged my daughter and I to sail away, offering his blessing—along with a gift card to splurge on pumpkin coffees.

At the outset of our journey, I felt shipwrecked.

The morning had been carefully planned: Jon was to drive us, by way of our truck, to the car-rental venue, saying goodbye once we were settled in our tiny, more fuel-efficient rental car.

We sailed into the rental car lot at 5 a.m. as planned, but the place was barren. Not one employee showed up, and the doors remained locked. I phoned two numbers: one had been disconnected, and the other went straight to voicemail. Maybe this was why I had received such a good rate.

I tapped my foot in the parking lot and kept eyeing the time. We were supposed to be on the road.

Finally, after standing around for over an hour, we decided that I would drive our truck instead. A far more expensive option, fuel-wise. But what other options did we have?

So we drove Jon back home, said our goodbyes, and took off. I immediately felt the morning's tension throbbing in my shoulders. We were now over two hours behind schedule. My plans had crumbled, and we had not even left our neighborhood, much less our state.

On the first leg of our two-day journey, I had planned to stop at my old college, excited to show Lauren the place where I had first laid eyes upon her father. I had planned to arrive on campus with plenty of extra time to wander the university bookstore and treat our daughter to a collegiate sweatshirt.

But now? The bookstore would be closed long before we arrived.

In the end it mattered not. What we needed were *not* campus sweatshirts, but unhurried hours of time together— time spent speaking truth into those tender crevices and heartaches. Our life in the pastoral fishbowl had taken a jagged turn, and the cruelty of others had scalded not only my husband but myself and our daughter, too.

It was soothing for me, as her mother, to understand our daughter's wounds, hear her worries, and have opportunity to respond in a gentle and unhurried way. Knowing that we would not make it to the bookstore, I slowed our trip, pausing from time to time. We wandered through Cracker Barrel and chose souvenirs of each state. We munched on lunch, unhurried and more relaxed in our travels.

The day that had begun as a shipwreck grew lovely— rounded out with the treat of hot pumpkin coffees, stunning roads teeming with autumn's golden splendor, and the cheer of road-trip playlists.

Eventually we arrived on campus and yes, the college bookstore was closed. So I played tour guide instead, first showing my girl the campus office where I had worked so long ago, followed by our dorms, the campus chapel, and the carefully tended grounds where her father and I had met. Little had changed, and I was most grateful that in a rapidly spinning world, this small piece of my history remained preserved.

This was an institution that at one time I had no intention of attending. My husband never would have landed there either if his acceptance paperwork had not been misplaced by another school. Such human error was the providential grace of God; it allowed us to meet and marry.

Standing on campus 28 years later, I felt aware of God's kindness again—the abundance of little ways in which he had magnificently colored my day, and my entire world.

Standing on the sidewalk of my alma mater, as the autumn breeze stirred, I watched Lauren shade her eyes against the early evening sun, hair glistening in fall's slowly descending sunbeams, taking in the athletic fields where her father had once spiraled the football.

She reminded me of my younger self. I had once been the grinning schoolgirl, proudly cheering from those stadium stands, my girlfriends elbowing me, our hearts happy on those magnificent fall days. It seemed like only yesterday, and yet here stood our youngest of four, now 18, walking precisely where her father and I once held hands. Back then neither of us were yet seasoned enough to even begin to appreciate the wonders and kindnesses of our heavenly Father.

A shiver descended my spine as in my mind's eye I observed the passage of time racing in reverse—seeing how God worked everything in his time to give me this moment with our daughter—and what I didn't know then I certainly appreciated now. My heart worshiped as I saw clearly God's unfathomably kind purposes fingerprinted upon our lives.

"I love it here, Mom," Lauren said, ocean-blue eyes twinkling: a girl on the cusp of her own college expedition at a different university yet held fast by the same heavenly Father who had kept me.

It was a beautiful moment.

And there was more: the unusual kindness of Jill, who had invited us in the first place.

We left our hotel bright and early on travel day number two, eager to meet my new friend face-to-face.

It was late afternoon when we swept into Jill's driveway, exhausted by two days of winding roads.

Lauren inspected her face in her pocket mirror, glanced at me, and laughed.

"Mom, can you believe we are about to stay with someone we have never met? Who would have guessed? This is so unlike us."

I grinned. She was spot on. Regardless, here we were.

Jill met us in the driveway. "Come on in," she beckoned with a wide and pretty smile, grabbing our luggage. "Jon is in the kitchen stirring the soup I made for dinner."

Jill's husband was every bit as welcoming as his wife, and their home was warm and comfortable. After we had settled our bags into the guest room, Jill invited us downstairs into their kitchen, where our dinner bubbled, smelling divine. While Jon stirred the pot, Jill chopped vegetables for the salad—husband and wife moving amicably about the kitchen—insisting that we relax in barstools situated at their spacious kitchen island. We nibbled a plate of appetizers arranged fetchingly on a plate: cubes of cheeses alongside cold cuts and fruit.

They asked questions and listened intently, welcoming us not only into their home but into their lives. As we chatted comfortably, as old friends would, I recognized this tender situation as something holy: strangers united through common faith. Our conversations moved quickly to the deep roots of our shared belief.

We had been invited over 1200 miles from home, chosen to join a warm campfire of friendship—a crackling blaze that served to mend our weary hearts.

⌒

The conference itself was a feast for the soul, and my late-night conversations with Jill, following the lectures, were a treasure. The day of our departure arrived much too soon, and Jill and Jon arose early in order to pack us a feast for our day's journey: tortillas wrapped tightly, holding a bed of bright Romaine lettuce, thinly sliced chicken, mayo, fine cheese, and tomato, as well as baggies containing crackers, fruit, and salted dark chocolates.

Yum.

Before we said our goodbyes, however, we were treated to a send-off feast for breakfast: yogurt, granola, muffins, and hot coffee. Jill asked all about Lauren's college plans, and I was not surprised in the least to discover the hours that Jill and Jon offer each week to teach young adult Sunday school classes at their church.

The conversation was food for our souls, which was precisely why we did not desire to leave. But the clock spoke otherwise.

My eyes filled as we hugged and waved goodbye. We had not even left their driveway when Lauren informed me that she could not remember a time when our family had been so sweetly treasured.

"It was wonderful, Mom. Can we come back?"

I had left for this trip exhausted: feeling worn down and wrung out. But the simple kindnesses and care of this godly woman had tempered the swollen ache within my soul—her extra measure of thoughtfulness breathing life to my bones and bringing a smile to my face.

Jill's homemade soup, coffee on a tray, hearty breakfasts, and a packed lunch for our return trip might seem insignificant, but they changed the way I understood kindness. Kindness need not be grand sweeping gestures or expensive gifts; it can just as easily be welcoming embraces and small thoughtful actions that soften the bumps of life.

Those cross-legged conversations late at night, the words shared over steaming mugs of tea as Jill nodded and listened—they healed me immeasurably. It was as though Christ was in that home, wrapping me up in a blanket of kindness—a refuge. It was as though the storms of difficulty receded for a while as I scooched close to the crackling fire—a warmth that whispered in gentle tones, "I see you, and you matter."

Remember there's no such thing as a small act of kindness. Every act creates a ripple with no logical end. (Scott Adams)

In Acts 27 and 28, the writer Luke tells us of an incident when the apostle Paul, along with 275 fellow shipmates, faced great difficulty at sea.

Paul was aboard the ship as a prisoner, en route to Rome to face trial for preaching about Jesus. The voyage did not start well. Paul warned against continuing, but the majority decided to press on. Then things got worse: "Soon a tempestuous wind, called the northeaster, struck down from the land. And when the ship was caught and could not face the wind, we gave way to it and were driven along" (Acts 27:14-15). The storm continued for days. The men began throwing the cargo overboard. "When neither sun nor stars appeared for many days, and no small tempest lay on us, all hope of our being saved was at last abandoned" (v 20).

But God had not forgotten his apostle. An angel appeared to Paul, telling him that he must not be afraid, because he was destined to stand before Caesar—and that in God's extravagant kindness, he had chosen to spare every man onboard with him.

Paul shared the angel's words with the men, informing them of the hard truth that they would eventually run aground on an island. And some two weeks after the storm started, they did: the ship eventually struck a reef a little way out from the shore.

The soldiers planned to kill the prisoners, so as to prevent their escape. But God's promise through the angel prevailed, and the centurion, wishing to save Paul's life, stopped them from murdering the prisoners. He ordered everyone who could swim to head for land, and those who could not to float on planks until they drifted to shore.

The tiny island was Malta, which in the Phoenician language means "a place of refuge."

The island natives welcomed this cluster of bedraggled, imprisoned men and soldiers to their land, kindling a fire to warm their guests, in the middle of cold, damp weather. It was, as Luke noted, an "*unusual* kindness" (28:2).

It must have been a great relief following the crew's marathon ordeal. I can imagine the hundreds floating or swimming to shore. As they struggled onto the beach, they must have felt frail, hungry, and cold. Suddenly, instead of finding themselves questioned suspiciously, they were graciously embraced by these perfect strangers, who built a beautifully roaring fire. How comforting that must have felt to their aching bones! I can imagine the soaking crew wrapping themselves in dry blankets, rubbing their hands together before the blaze, blowing into their cupped hands, while reaching for a warmed cup of water and nourishment.

The first night, Paul, while gathering wood for the fire, was bitten by a viper. The natives waited for him to swell and die, as any victim would, speculating that Paul must be out of favor with the gods. Yet when Paul boldly carried on—shaking the snake into the fire and suffering no ill effects—the Maltans were amazed. They suddenly flipped their script, now assuming he must be a god.

In time, Paul went to the house of Publius, who was a Roman chief of the island. He too was unusually kind, extending generous hospitality to the group for three whole days (v 7). Publius' father was sick; Paul prayed for him, laid hands on him, and he was healed. The good news spread quickly. Soon all the island people who suffered disease approached Paul and were cured. They trusted Paul, and perhaps some came to a saving faith in Christ.

The shipwrecked crew remained as guests in Malta for three months. Ninety days for God to clearly display his kindness in gifting Paul with rest, and in gifting a glimpse of the gospel to these islanders. You see, God had a purpose in the catastrophes at sea. When all hope seemed lost, he brought the men onto an island where only he knew they would be treated with such generosity, given a respite, as Paul healed bodies and souls. The gospel had to be preached in Rome, and God ensured that Paul was given all he needed to get there.

God knows that we are frail creatures of dust. He permits suffering for his holy purpose, but he also graces us with times to rest and recharge.

After several months, when the next ship arrived to pick up the crew and sail to Rome, the island people honored the men, graciously stocking their ship with all necessities, going above and beyond.

It reminds me of Jill.

Kindness should be blossoming in the life of every sincere believer. Perhaps God will use us, like the Maltans, to bless one of his servants in need. May we be about the good work of building warm and welcoming fires, wordlessly expressing: "I see you shivering in the cold. Come by the fire I have made and warm yourself."

The church is to be a place of refuge, unusually kind in the midst of life's tempests. This is the heartbeat of God himself—going to the greatest of lengths in a bleak, dark, stormy world: sending his beloved Son to die that we might live. What seemed the darkest day in history was actually its brightest point, leading to our rescue. Is there anything kinder?

Are you recognizing the warmth of God's kindness upon your face even in those countless small and precious moments today? This week? This month? Consider all of those little road-trip moments of life, gifted to you by your Father's gracious hand.

If you are a sincere Christian, your kindness to others is not a performance, a duty to check off. Rather, it radiates from the blazing fire inside of your soul—flames fueled by the Holy Spirit, who points us to trust and obey God, through Jesus Christ.

Sometimes we wrongly assume that kindness must be flashy and expensive—a knock-it-out-of-the-park-type of showy goodwill.

But biblically? Genuine kindness toward others, as seen in Acts 28, is as simple as a warm fire, a welcoming spirit, a tasty meal, or the filling up of a sojourner's pantry.

And Jesus says that as we do these things, we serve the Savior himself:

When the Son of Man comes in his glory, and all the angels with him, then he will sit on his glorious throne. Before him will be gathered all the nations, and he will separate people one from another as a shepherd separates the sheep from the goats. And he will place the sheep on his right, but the goats on the left.

Then the King will say to those on his right, "Come, you who are blessed by my Father, inherit the kingdom prepared for you from the foundation of the world. For I was hungry and you gave me food, I was thirsty and you gave me drink, I was a stranger and you welcomed me, I was naked and you clothed me, I was sick and you visited me, I was in prison and you came to me."

Then the righteous will answer him, saying, "Lord, when did we see you hungry and feed you, or thirsty and give you drink? And when did we see you a stranger and welcome you, or naked and clothe you? And when did we see you sick or in prison and visit you?" And the King will answer them, "Truly, I say to you, as you did it to one of the least of these my brothers, you did it to me." (Matthew 25:31–40)

Unusual kindness today is pressing into and obeying the prompting of the Holy Spirit, moment by moment. It is going a step further in thinking less of ourselves, and more of others. It is simple acts of generosity, done as though we were serving Jesus himself.

SIX

Goodness: Uprightness of Heart and Life

"He has told you, O man, what is good: and what
does the LORD require of you but to do justice, and to
love kindness, and to walk humbly with your God?"
(Micah 6:8)

To begin, I must tell you three things.

First of all, despite his average stature, my grandfather was the tallest, sturdiest, and most upright tree of my childhood.

Second, the Greek word for goodness, used in the list of the fruit of the Spirit in Galatians 5, is *agathosune*, meaning uprightness of heart and life.

Third?

My grandfather was goodness, in spades.

I was six years old and the world had opened in magnificent and stunning blossoms—a brilliant garden of possibilities before me.

I had learned to read.

Suddenly, I was able to unlock meaning in street signs, billboards, and most importantly, *books*.

These gifts of consonants and vowels, paired with a heavy-duty manilla library card, yielded my passport to new worlds. The surprising delight in unfamiliar words and pronunciations, and the joy of easy reader books, invited me to imaginative, faraway places even while I remained seated at my first-grade desk.

That Christmas, Grandpa gifted me *The Webster's Dictionary for Children*, the only request on my list. My uncle was stunned by my simple wish, wide-eyed, and harping with: "What first grader asks for a dictionary? This isn't normal." He hovered at my mother's elbow, agitated. "I think she should see the pediatrician."

Grandpa did not poke fun. "Of course you require a dictionary!" he smiled good-naturedly. "We readers must stick together." He gently elbowed me as I hugged my dictionary, my eyes dancing, treasuring my perfect present.

Grandpa had gifted me the world. Spellings, pronunciations, and definitions were now at my fingertips. I gobbled it up, a student of words, eager and greedy to learn.

One afternoon I skipped down my grandparents' basement stairs, and meandered over to Grandpa's desk, studying the dozens of pens and pencils and keychains displayed neatly upon the desk. Grandpa's job involved selling customized promotional products to businesses, and he was continuously receiving new samples to add to his collection.

My eyes landed upon a new paperweight. It was unique—a solid half-sphere of glass with a prominent question mark imprinted within the center. Around the outer edges I carefully read the words:

Who is Bob Gardner?

Picking up the paperweight, I was surprised by its heaviness in my hands. I studied it and considered the answer to the question.

"Bob Gardner is my grandpa, and the best one in the entire world." My heart swelled.

"Just think," I told myself, "out of all the grandfathers in the world, God made him mine!"

I was proud to know who Bob Gardner was: a good man, respected by his customers, loved by his neighbors and friends, and adored by his family.

That solid paperweight reflected the sturdiness of Grandpa's virtues. Bob Gardner was a Micah 6:8 man: kind and humble and just—a triumvirate that precious few can claim, but which is God's very definition of goodness:

> *He has told you, O man, what is good: and what*
> *does the LORD require of you but to do justice, and to*
> *love kindness, and to walk humbly with your God?*
> *(Micah 6:8)*

These character traits are God's way of forming a braided cord of goodness, strong and lovely—a likeness of the heart of God.

Who was Bob Gardner?

A kind man.

Decades have passed, and I can still resurrect the smell of Grandpa's basement office—a slim yet neat space that he shared only with the washing machine and dryer. My grandmother's laundry detergent, fresh and clean, permeated the air as the clothing and towels spun. Grandpa's office swirled not only with the fine fragrance of detergent, but of paper—reams of it stacked neatly on a shelf. That plus the scent of his *Old Spice* aftershave.

Nowadays it occurs to me that the clunking noise of the dryer must have been a nuisance as he phoned his many customers. If it did bother him, he never complained. My grandmother worked as a secretary, which meant that Grandpa, who worked from home decades before such a thing was common, was tasked with slinging the damp washing into the dryer. I can see him even now, a classy wool beanie warming his balding head, two space heaters aimed at his desk chair, as he cheerfully walked from his work space to tend to the laundry.

Many times the clothing Grandpa laundered belonged to my family. Until I was twelve, my parents, brother, and I dwelt 45 minutes away from my grandparents, in an ancient New England farmhouse—a structure that had been neatly divided into four pocket-sized apartments: dwellings without the benefit of a washer and dryer.

My father, who worked nearby my grandparents' house, occasionally dropped by their home, in the pitch dark of morning, to start a load of laundry prior to work. But it was my grandfather who, upon finishing his daily egg and toast breakfast, transferred our whites to the dryer and started the basketful of dark clothing before turning his attention back to his work.

No chore was beneath him.

Ever.

In fact, no kindness, however small, was beneath him.

Grandpa was a fine salesman. My brother and I enjoyed sitting at the top of those basement office steps as our grandfather worked, our small elbows resting on our knees with our hands cupping our chins. We were spies surveying Grandpa's good deeds as he phoned his customers. He worked from a rolling chair, the phone cord stretching long as he wheeled himself over to his filing cabinets, plucking catalogs from his drawers, listening as clients explained their promotional wishes.

People trusted Grandpa, and it showed. He traveled the extra mile with ease: "How is that new grandson of yours, Bill? What's that? Still in an incubator? I am sorry to hear this." Or: "I have been thinking of you, Michael. How was Anne's surgery? Do you need anything?"

Then, promptly after hanging up the phone, he reached for the thick Yellow Pages phone book, glasses low on his nose as his index finger searched for the correct number. He then phoned a local chocolatier and florist, delivering tangible well-wishes to the families of his customers.

That accomplished, he swiveled his chair around, smiling broadly, beckoning to my brother and me.

"I thought I heard my grandchildren!"

We scampered down the stairs and pulled open the heaviest metal drawer in the cabinet, which was full of trinkets—bright, fun, and quirky items. Letter openers, stress-balls, flashlights, key chains, coin purses, mugs, pins, juice glasses, teeny tiny pads of paper, ash trays, pencils, shoulder bags, and can openers. We were generously allowed to look and touch nearly everything.

He was kind like that.

Who was Bob Gardner?

A humble man.

My grandpa had relinquished his life to the Lord as a young husband and father—a 30-something year-old man—upon hearing the gospel at a Billy Graham crusade. Grandpa turned away from his sinful life and ran to Christ, immediately surrendering his entire being to God.

By all accounts his life changed dramatically afterwards. The old Bob Gardner had vanished, along with his smoking, drinking, and gambling ways. He became a brand new person.

As a little girl I never grew weary of hearing his salvation story. When he spoke of the crusade, tears sprang up in his eyes, and he inevitably removed his glasses, dabbing his eyes with his handkerchief, and smiling.

"The grace of God," he said, shaking his head, unashamed.

Grandpa found a church for his young family and planted himself under solid Bible teaching. He served faithfully in that same congregation for decades, as both a trustee and an usher. Grandpa read his Bible and checked off each page as he went along. He spoke often of the way the psalms ministered to his spirit through the writings of King David—a ruler who, like him, had been forgiven of many sins, and yet was a man after God's own heart.

The grace of God made Grandpa humble. He understood that God alone is good, and that any small crumbs of goodness within himself were the marks of the Holy Spirit at work.

If there was one thing Grandpa could not tolerate, it was a braggart. "What does he want? A medal or a chest to pin it on?" was his famous saying for anyone arrogant enough to seek and demand his own praise.

One Sunday, Grandpa and Grandma visited our church. Our pastor and his family of seven lived in a narrow parsonage directly attached to a converted barn, which at one point served as the church sanctuary. Their furniture, clothing, and earthly goods were scant, at best. Grandpa quietly noted our minister's threadbare suit jacket, dress pants, and tired-looking shoes. (How he admired finely polished shoes!)

Grandpa went home that day, simmering, quiet, and determined, and soon hatched a plan to discreetly obtain our pastor's measurements. He then went shopping, and purchased two costly suits, and had them delivered anonymously to our pastor's home, so as not to embarrass or offend. I was sworn to absolute secrecy, which made the entire event wonderfully thrilling.

To see the humility of my grandfather in action—desiring no recognition or thanks, continuously considering others more important than himself—was a precious jewel.

And then, to observe my pastor standing behind the pulpit the next Sunday, seeming a bit taller in his fine new attire, changed me too. I glimpsed the wonderful impact that doing good to others from a place of tender humility could have.

I understood the secret to Grandpa's magic, and it wasn't magic at all. It was Christ at work within him. Grandpa placed all of his confidence in his Savior, and it showed.

Who was Bob Gardner?

He was kind and humble.

And he was just.

You see, the essence of goodness is more than kindness and humility alone. Goodness also includes justice.

One afternoon at a family gathering, I overheard my grandfather informing my parents and aunts and uncles that someone had been caught with sticky hands at church, pilfering from the offering plates.

The guilty man was greatly humiliated. He was a church member who had served as an usher for quite some time. Now caught in his sin, he hung his head in deep shame and embarrassment, finally admitting that he had been stealing cash from the collection plate for years.

Later on, a family friend filled my mother in on the rest of the saga. I stood on the fringes, circling around my mother's skirt as little girls are wont to do. I caught the entire conversation, golden words that sparkled and danced, revealing the essence of Grandpa's character.

The words still spin in my memory, decades after they were spoken.

"Bob Gardner is the measure of kindness and justice. That usher will have to repay every penny of what he stole, but it was your father who confronted him and then worked out a quiet way to keep him from prison, preserving his dignity with forgiveness and a reasonable repayment plan. Your father is a good man."

Who was Bob Gardner?

He was goodness in spades, I tell you. A giant redwood, a magnificent tree in the forest of Christendom. He lived justly, loved kindness, and walked humbly with his God. Grandpa was certainly not perfect—he struggled with a quick temper, for instance, rising up in defense of his loved ones—and yet he was made new by Christ, forgiven and free, devoted to God, and filled to the brim with the fruit of the Holy Spirit.

A man after God's own heart.

Have you ever considered the biblical benchmark for goodness?

Ponder again God's directive in Micah 6:8:

> *He has told you, O man, what is good; and what*
> *does the LORD require of you but to do justice, and to*
> *love kindness, and to walk humbly with your God?*
> *(Micah 6:8)*

Justice. Kindness. Humility. Remove any of these three, and goodness evaporates.

The Pharisees of Jesus' day were decent, law-abiding citizens who claimed to walk justly. They kept all God's laws to the letter and sought to ensure other people did too—or so they thought. Yet they were void of goodness, because they walked in pride rather than humility, without offering a tender-hearted kindness toward others: "They tie up heavy burdens, hard to bear, and lay them on people's shoulders," said Jesus, "but they themselves are not willing to move them with their finger. They do all their deeds to be seen by others" (Matthew 23:4-5). Jesus called them hypocrites; white-washed tombs full of dead man's bones, filthy on the inside (v 27). Clearly, they were not good men, despite obeying so many of the strict Old Testament laws (v 23).

How about the rich young ruler? Three of the Gospel-writers relate his encounter with Jesus. Matthew tells us that he was young (Matthew 19:20); Luke tells us that he was a ruler (Luke 18:18); all three tell us that he was rich.

Yet he comes to Jesus with a question:

> *"Good Teacher, what must I do to inherit eternal life?" And Jesus said to him, "Why do you call me good? No one is good except God alone. You know the commandments: 'Do not murder, Do not commit adultery, Do not steal, Do not bear false witness, Do not defraud, Honor your father and mother.'" And he said to him, "Teacher, all these I have kept from my youth." (Mark 10:17-20)*

Here is a man who earnestly desires goodness, and who considers Jesus to be a "Good Teacher." If he really had kept God's commandments since his youth, that would have made him a kind and just ruler. Yet Jesus wants to show him that his goodness does not run as deep as he thinks it does.

> *And Jesus, looking at him, loved him, and said to him, "You lack one thing: go, sell all that you have and give to the poor, and you will have treasure in heaven; and come, follow me." Disheartened by the saying, he went away sorrowful, for he had great possessions. (Mark 10:21-22)*

The man's lack of humility surfaced when he failed to pass the test of genuine surrender, by refusing to give away the one thing Jesus asked him to part with: his riches. Jesus was inviting him to a life of inner wealth: forsaking all to follow Jesus completely. The man walked away in refusal, full of sorrow, unwilling to humble himself—choosing earthly possessions over eternal treasure. Goodness was not within him.

By way of contrast, it is fascinating to consider the goodness of King David, who we're told was a "man after [God's] heart" (Acts 13:22). What made him such?

One cursory glance at 2 Samuel 11 – 12 proves that he was a man undone by his own grievous sins of deceit, murder, and adultery. A world away from Micah 6:8! And yet he was favored by God. How was this even possible?

It's because after being confronted with his sin—his complete failure to do good—he turned back to God in utter repentance. This is what separated him from the law-abiding, cold-hearted Pharisees and the prideful rich young ruler, who heeded neither Jesus' warnings nor his invitation. But David truly loved and feared God, and returned to the Lord, broken and contrite. We see that most vividly in Psalm 51, which he wrote in the aftermath of one of his greatest failures:

> *Have mercy on me, O God, according to your steadfast love; according to your abundant mercy blot out my transgressions.*
>
> *Wash me thoroughly from my iniquity, and cleanse me from my sin!*
>
> *For I know my transgressions, and my sin is ever before me.*
>
> *Against you, you only, have I sinned and done what is evil in your sight, so that you may be justified in your words and blameless in your judgment.*
>
> *(Psalm 51:1-4)*

Like King David, we all fall short of goodness in daily living. Our good heavenly Father sent Jesus for this very problem: sin. We are able to repent, turning away from sin as we humbly acknowledge our wrongdoing before the Lord, and are washed by the one who is God's goodness and loving kindness personified: Jesus Christ. Titus 3:3-7 tells us:

> *For we ourselves were once foolish, disobedient, led astray, slaves to various passions and pleasures, passing our days in malice and envy, hated by others and hating one another. But when the goodness*

and loving kindness of God our Savior appeared,
he saved us, not because of works done by us in
righteousness, but according to his own mercy, by the
washing of regeneration and renewal of the Holy
Spirit, whom he poured out on us richly through
Jesus Christ our Savior, so that being justified by his
grace we might become heirs according to the hope of
eternal life.

Oh, the beauty of this passage! Do you see it clearly? The goodness of God rescued us from our sins and from God's wrath! Jesus came to earth to save us when we were not good. He saved us because we were hopelessly wicked, apart from him. He alone is good, and we are incapable of slogging our way to righteousness through our own futile attempts at goodness. Only a genuine faith in Christ will soften our hearts, as he renews us by the Holy Spirit.

Such tenderness of spirit will enable us to diligently devote ourselves to good works, for the benefit of others. For that is where repentance leads, as the very next verse tells us:

The saying is trustworthy, and I want you to insist
on these things, so that those who have believed in
God may be careful to devote themselves to good
works. These things are excellent and profitable for
people. (v 8)

Our good God saved us when we were not good so that we might *be* good and *do* good. Likewise, in Matthew 5:16 Jesus reminds us:

*Let your light shine before others, so that they may
see your good works and give glory to your Father
who is in heaven.*

Goodness always involves the visible. Showing kindness, walking in humility, and meting out justice are outward acts performed from a sincere heart.

As those saved by God, we claim the name "Christian," meaning *belonging to the anointed one.*

To be anointed is to be set apart by God for a purpose. And just as Christ was anointed so too are we—to illuminate not ourselves, but our Maker. We are set apart to do good.

*For we are his workmanship, created in Christ Jesus
for good works, which God prepared beforehand, that
we should walk in them. (Ephesians 2:10)*

Ask yourself…

Am I displaying the braided cord of goodness: kindness, humility, and justice?

How am I practicing daily kindness in those small acts to others?

Am I humble before God and man, or am I seeking to grandstand? Am I putting my desires front and center; seeking to make my own name great?

Am I searching for ways to act justly, with godly wisdom, bringing God's word to life through right actions and responses?

Have you ever had the opportunity to stand in front of a magnificent stained-glass cathedral window as the sunlight dances through the array of brightly colored glass?

What happens as the light streams in?

The colors glisten and sparkle upon your clothing. The patterns are not nearly as bright as the panes of colored glass itself—but your shirt is no longer plain, is it? You now reflect the colors of the stained-glass window.

Our fruit of goodness is like those pretty colors flickering on our shirt. God, like the sunbeam, sets his gaze upon his own children. As Christ-followers, God sees us through the window pane of Jesus, who, like the lovely stained glass, is steeped in rich arrays of perfect color. We have been forgiven by faith in our crucified and risen Savior, and the image of Christ is imprinted upon our frames, showing up in our acts of goodness.

If you love God, he now sees you only through the blood of his Son. God loves you, and is making you look more and more like Jesus. The deeper your roots of faith grow as you trust not in yourself, but in God, the brighter your own clothing becomes as the stained glass lights your clothing. Your goodness is found in Christ Jesus, alone.

My grandfather's uprightness of heart and life were nothing that he mustered of his own accord. They were the stained-glass goodness of Christ, reflected in him.

And it showed up brightly on his clothing for all of the world to see.

SEVEN

Faithfulness: Fidelity to the Finish Line

"Let us hold fast the confession of our hope without wavering, for he who promised is faithful."
(Hebrews 10:23)

It was a warm summer afternoon, and shortly after schlepping a gazillion boxes into our new home, I was spent. I had painted three rooms in as many days, and had speckled hands and aching muscles as proof of my labors. In addition to painting, I had unpacked many of the aforementioned boxes, while shuffling furniture hither and yon.

I was pining for a breather.

Leashing up one of our dogs, I stepped into the sunshine and stretched my legs while fueling my lungs with a burst of fresh air. As I ambled down our curvy driveway, I felt a shiver of delight at the prospect of exploring our new neighborhood. It was deeply invigorating to take a break and enjoy the great outdoors.

I had not gone far when I spotted an older couple down the road, fetching their mail, as their Basset Hound sniffed the air. Waving a friendly hello, I had intended to keep walking, when the woman asked if I had just moved into the house on the hill.

I nodded and as our dogs greeted each other, tails humming, we began chatting.

"My name is Ginny," she said, extending her hand. Her voice was robust; clear. I liked her immediately.

Here is what I did not yet know: God was answering my long-standing prayer for a wise Christian mentor. After years of pleading, I had nearly given up asking God for a mature Christian friend.

Here I was, a woman in my late forties, and a soon-to-be-empty-nester, standing at the brink of a difficult change. Ginny, in her mid-seventies, had already walked the path I was now beginning. God heard my pleas and in his exquisite timing blessed me with this new friend to teach me something new about faithfulness.

The truly faithful are few, aren't they? I tremble as I observe old friends, extended family, and even dear church members falling away from what had once appeared to be authentic biblical faith. With each falling away, I consider what Matthew 7:13-14 tells us: "Enter by the narrow gate. For the gate is wide and the way is easy that leads to destruction, and those who enter by it are many. For the gate is narrow and the way is hard that leads to life, and those who find it are few." Lord, how I want to follow that narrow path all the way.

Soon after our initial meeting, Ginny contacted me, asking me to join her women's Bible study, which she has been facilitating for many years. I gladly accepted her warm invitation.

That was several years ago, and since then I have regularly jumped deep into the well of Scripture with these kind ladies, mining the depths of God's word as we meet to learn and pray and hold each other accountable to God's word. Ginny guides our group, welcoming us with her generous smile, while keeping us on pace with meaty, biblical questions.

And something else I soon discovered? These women have their own beautiful stories of Ginny's faithfulness. On countless occasions she has invited them to attend Bible study, cooked them a meal, or called simply to encourage, holding them up in prayer.

Ginny takes God's word, studies it, then practices it, opening her home in hospitality, sharing recipes and books and gifts with others. Her fidelity to God overflows—a movie reel of humble servanthood.

If you met Ginny today, you might guess she was nearing 70, when in fact, she is almost 80. In the final season of life when many are content to sit back in their easy chair and scroll their phones, or become lost in soaking up the news, Ginny is disinterested in such pastimes. In fact, last summer while she was recuperating from a medical procedure, I dropped by and she welcomed me from the sofa with her usual, "Hi, Honey Bunny!" as she happily knit scarves for a local ministry.

She plays the piano each Sunday morning at church, cooks up spaghetti dinners for her entire church family, organizes fundraisers, and perpetually serves the body of Christ in numerous, hidden ways, void of all fanfare.

Faithfulness is not a robe that Ginny dons for show, nor is it a string of benevolent, yet futile attempts to earn favor from God, but it is the fabric of her soul. Her life is an outflow of her faithfulness to Christ. And her deeply embedded roots are continuing to stretch and flourish, producing more and more ripe, lavish fruit as she ages. The Holy Spirit has flooded this dear friend of mine, and the golden outflow of her faithfulness blesses everyone in her orbit.

Perhaps reading that description tempts part of you to despair: "I'll never be like her!" But lest you imagine that Ginny's faithfulness is simply a character trait sweetly woven into her personality from birth, please know that it is the Holy Spirit who is at work in and through this woman. God has shaped and transformed Ginny from the inside out, stretching and increasing her faithfulness, mainly by way of suffering.

Godly saints usually have a backstory of learning to suffer well, don't they? It's always been that way. Peter tells his readers that they are being "grieved by various trials, so that the tested genuineness of your faith—more precious than gold that perishes though it is tested by fire—may be found to result in praise and glory and honor at the revelation of Jesus Christ" (1 Peter 1:6-7). It is almost impossible to develop a resilient faith without first being tested by hot fires.

And Ginny has been molded in the inferno.

Twenty-five years ago, Ginny was in her mid-fifties, an empty nester, and employed as a public-school counselor. One day the headmaster of a local Christian preschool approached her.

The small school was in desperate need of a new director, as enrollment had dipped and enthusiasm had plummeted. Swift change was called for, and he believed Ginny was the perfect candidate to revive the preschool.

Ginny accepted the position, taking a significant pay cut, and quickly made smart improvements, such as introducing a rich Christian curriculum and adding a kindergarten program. New cleaning protocols and other simple updates were put in place, and the little school began to blossom. Ginny's charm was magnetic, and word spread.

The number of students increased steadily over the course of the next few years, swelling from 100 to 400, as Ginny added qualified, Christian staff and organized fundraising galas in order to fund the purchase of a new outdoor jungle gym and plush, indoor carpeting.

Ginny added one grade per year until the school offered programs from infant-aged through fifth grade. Under her careful stewardship, the school gained accreditation following a period of intense scrutiny. Parents were thrilled, the church was encouraged, and Ginny was considered a treasure amongst the staff and students.

There was only one problem.

The headmaster grew jealous of Ginny's accomplishments. He resented her success, he despised her easy camaraderie with the staff and parents, and he was incensed by the accolades given to her by the community.

And then came a shocking discovery.

The headmaster had been misappropriating school funds for years. It was tricky, as his guilt could not be proven without litigation, and that would cause the school to fall to pieces. When the truth came to light, Ginny was one of the few who knew the ugly truth. She was grieved to learn that the school she loved and served was $50,000 in debt.

While attempting to unearth a solution, Ginny fell ill with shingles, likely due to the heavy stress she was shouldering. She missed one entire week of work, and the timing could not have been worse.

Longing to stay faithful to God and the school, she typed her staff a two-page document from her sickbed, asking them to drop to their knees in prayer over the many difficulties now surrounding them. She wrote with clarity: "Satan is alive and well and attacking our precious Christian school."

When Ginny recovered and returned to work, the headmaster called her into his office.

He was livid.

"What are you doing?" he raged. "I don't believe in Satan, and he is certainly not working at our school. Why would you ever say such things to our staff?"

"Because it is the truth," Ginny answered.

What was happening? The headmaster did not believe in Satan? Had he not even read his Bible? What would she do now?

For months the war quietly raged. This man began roadblocking Ginny at every turn, whispering lies and gossip. He thwarted her attempts to make further school improvements and grew enraged with every blessing that God poured out.

Ginny pieced together a beautiful fundraiser, in record time, with the audacious goal of raising $50,000 in one evening, in an attempt to pay the massive school debt incurred by the headmaster. The families within the student body and the church rose to the occasion, and the goal was miraculously reached that night.

Ginny forged ahead, faithfully, leading her staff on a weekend retreat, inviting them to draw near to Christ through two days of personal prayer time and Scripture meditation.

They returned to school the following Monday, noticeably refreshed, and eager to serve.

Thank you, Ginny. We needed this.

Such strength and unity, inspired by Ginny's faithful commitment to God, infuriated the headmaster.

The final straw came after Ginny single-handedly organized a cooking palooza, serving 800 people, in celebration of the school's 25th anniversary. Her dedication to the school and the Lord was unmistakable, and she openly gave God the glory for the success of this institution. A school that had been on the verge of extinction was now thriving, growing, and making disciples, and was wonderfully debt-free.

Envy and jealousy and bitterness had darkened the heart of the headmaster. The headmaster turned his rage against Ginny in staff meetings, but never in front of parents or students. His angst ultimately surged to the point that Ginny knew she could no longer stay.

As she told me the story, she paused and said, "Remember, wherever God is moving, so is Satan. But also remember this: our God is always faithful. He had me there for a specific time. I prayed, and God granted me peace to retire."

When she informed the headmaster, telling him that one of them needed to leave, he sneered, saying they would have to throw her a going-away party.

Ginny declined. "It is not about me," she said simply. "This is God's school."

His response? *I hate it when you do that.*

The teachers made her a lovely goodbye quilt and threw a celebration in honor of her six years of faithful service. The changes had been monumental, and hundreds of children and their families had benefited. Most people remained unaware that Ginny and her husband were having to move away and step into retirement earlier than planned. The headmaster, still enraged, slandered her from afar for years, suddenly accusing her of misusing school funds—a bogus claim without an iota of merit. He accused her of his own secret crimes.

Ginny unpacked their belongings in their new home and started again. She immediately busied herself serving in their new church, where she is still active today, decades later.

I recently asked her: "How did you stay close to the Lord without growing bitter?"

"I clung to Romans 8:28," she said, before quoting it to me: "'And we know that for those who love God all things work together for good, for those who are called according to his purpose.'"

And that is the cry of the faithful—holding fast to God each day, come what may. God's faithful play the long game. They understand that personal faithfulness to God depends on his nature: God is faithfully stitching all things together for our good.

Faith is the assurance of things hoped for, the conviction of things not seen. (Hebrews 11:1)

Faithfulness is the act of remaining steadfast, trusting fully in our invisible Maker. Each one of God's children is called to persevere—to run the race of life to the finish line.

Faithfulness does not save us: God does. But faithfulness does reveal that we *have been saved*, doesn't it?

As Christians, we long to hold fast! But how do we yield to the Holy Spirit, allowing him to accomplish this in and through us? How do we live in a state of God-honoring fidelity to life's end, despite our ongoing sin, our imperfections, and life's many hardships?

Chapter 10 of Hebrews is an invigorating reminder of how to remain faithful:

Therefore, brothers, since we have confidence to enter the holy places by the blood of Jesus, by the new and living way that he opened for us through the curtain, that is, through his flesh, and since we have a great priest over the house of God, let us draw near with a true heart in full assurance of faith, with our hearts sprinkled clean from an evil conscience and

*our bodies washed with pure water. Let us hold fast
the confession of our hope without wavering, for he
who promised is faithful. And let us consider how
to stir up one another to love and good works, not
neglecting to meet together, as is the habit of some,
but encouraging one another, and all the more as you
see the Day drawing near. (Hebrews 10:19-25)*

This small passage holds the three keys to faithfulness,
birthed from the blood of Jesus.

Draw near, hold fast, and stir up.

Draw near.

The Lord desires fellowship with his children.
Through the death and resurrection of Jesus, we now
have direct access to God and can come to him through
prayer and the reading of Scripture. Drawing near to
God is often made complicated when in reality, it is
beautifully simple.

Get close to God by praying every day, speaking
directly with your heavenly Father, who hears you.
Remind yourself that you are a new creation by faith
in Jesus. Praise him for his goodness, thank him for
his faithfulness, and ask him to grow your faith in him,
moment-by-moment. Determine to take the Bible seri-
ously, carving out daily time to read and meditate on
Scripture, which is God's voice to us. And then? Obey
him. When you sin, as we all do, confess and apologize
with a soft, humble heart, returning to his presence. It
really is that simple.

And if you're earnestly seeking to do those things, however imperfectly: take heart. Though they may look and feel very ordinary, God will work through them.

Hold fast.

Holding fast to the confession of our hope without wavering (Hebrews 10:23) means a stubborn stick-to-it-ness. It says, *God will not break his promises; so I will not break trust.* Such determination is gifted to the believer by our faithful God, who grows our faith. Later in the chapter the writer of Hebrews warns us with the idea in reverse: "But we are not of those who shrink back and are destroyed, but of those who have faith and preserve their souls" (v 39). To hold fast is the opposite of shrinking back, isn't it?

Holding fast is like hugging a tall, sturdy tree during a torrential, windy storm. That tree, old and mighty, has long, powerful roots that stretch underground, anchoring it to the earth. The tree weathers all gusts, remaining sturdy and upright, and we borrow its strength, clutching our arms and legs around it, holding fast while the winds blow.

How much stronger is God in our times of trial than even the sturdiest tree? He is faithful, always, and our faithfulness of heart and deed is rooted in his steadfastness.

Stir up others to love and good works.

The author of Hebrews urges us to consistently meet together and encourage one another in biblical truth. The day of Christ's return is drawing near, and the only way we'll hold on in faith until then is to hold on together.

Resolve to be the faithful one who chooses not to forsake meeting together, knowing that the church is called to gather regularly. Our souls are desperate to be continually nourished by the preaching of God's word and the encouragement of God's people. As the body of Christ, we need to stir up one another, poking and prodding each other toward love and truth and good deeds.

A faithful commitment to serve your local church body will strengthen the entire flock. How? Perhaps with a kind word, or a pat on the back, or even a simple, "How are you today?" followed by a patient, listening ear. May we happily take the time to embark on a conversation reminding one another of the goodness of the sermon message. May we be faithful to show up and live the gospel.

Sadly, it has become the cultural norm to attend church only occasionally. This is not God's plan. We will miss many opportunities to strengthen and serve others, as well as opportunities to be strengthened and served ourselves. We need to be regularly reminded that God is faithful; and faithfulness to him looks like being a faithful friend to his people.

"Am I faithful?"

In one sense that question cannot be answered in the present: it is time which serves as proof of who we are. The question is this: will you—will I—stay the course?

It is helpful to imagine the Christian life as a marathon. The apostle Paul did:

Do you not know that in a race all the runners run,
but only one receives the prize? So run that you may
obtain it. (1 Corinthians 9:24)

Our personal race will certainly contain seasons when bright, golden sunshine warms our faces as we run along the narrow way. We close our eyes, faces tilted upward, smiling and squinting into the golden light. Sipping cool water, limbs warm and loose, we feel the goodness of God through his visible kindnesses to us. Church is vibrant. Friendships blossom and family seems kind. Our hearts beat healthy, vibrant, and strong, and our work is both enjoyable and profitable. Bills are paid, our goals are on track, and life's course is pulsing, steady, and sure beneath our feet.

As we continue our marathon, the skies abruptly change. Clouds begin to accumulate, dimming the sun's rays. A soft rain falls, the drizzle turns chilly and cold, and soon our clothing is soaked and our shoes are soggy, uncomfortable in their heaviness. In these darker legs of our journey, friendships diminish with little warning, and relationships grow distant and lukewarm. Church is frustrating or painful. Our work seems unsatisfying, creating a listless apathy within our spirits. We are abandoned by family; our differences swelling and producing an insurmountable barrier. And to make everything worse? We are now jogging on an uphill path. Our muscles are slow and weak, tightened by the rain's chill.

Stay the course, dear Christian. There is a torch in your hand—a flame that alights. It is the Holy Spirit, interceding on our behalf, pointing us to Christ. And as the flame burns steadily, we turn back to him, again and again. One step, one act of obedience at a time. We do not need to look into tomorrow, or next week or next year. We run our race one small step at a time. And those steps eventually stretch into days, weeks, months, and years. One moment stacked upon another. We persevere in faith because the God who calls us is faithful.

What do the faithful hold in common?

They finish well, facing each hurdle, eyes on Christ in full assurance, guided by the Holy Spirit, running the race of faith to the end: stumbling sometimes but never giving up. Because although we may falter, God is unwavering in his faithfulness, and he calls us to follow him to the finish line.

I pause and imagine Ginny, leaping into eternity, crossing the finish line, skipping on streets of pure gold, her smile bright as she calls to me.

"Come on, Honeybunny! Stay faithful to God! You are almost home!"

And there we will dwell with our faithful Savior. He has promised.

EIGHT

Gentleness: Humble Strength

*"Brothers, if anyone is caught in any transgression,
you who are spiritual should restore him in a spirit of
gentleness. Keep watch on yourself,
lest you too be tempted."
(Galatians 6:1)*

I was three months graduated from college, newly married, and seeking to grow roots in an unfamiliar part of the country. In the middle of unpacking our modest belongings—along with wedding gifts that now seemed much too fancy for our pocket-sized apartment—I received a phone call to say that I had been hired as a receptionist for a local Christian-based company.

I smiled as my husband gave me a celebratory hug. While deeply grateful for the work, I felt the burden of one more weight to add to my growing pile of adjustments.

One week later my shiny wedding band sparkled in the morning sun as I grabbed my bagged lunch and made my way to our apartment's parking lot, ready to embark on day one of work.

We had one car, and now two jobs. Jon would drop me off on one side of town before making his way to the opposite side of town for his work.

Florida's sun, which had once seemed brilliant and hopeful and endlessly happy, now felt insufferable—oppressive. I was not accustomed to year-round heat and humidity. It is one thing to vacation in the south, but another thing entirely to call it home. I was just figuring this out. My hair had wilted in the short journey from apartment to car, and sweat pooled at the back of my neck.

It certainly did not help that I was nervous. As Jon drove, I mentally rehashed the events of the past month: a wedding, a honeymoon, a 1300-mile move south, a new church, a new job, and truthfully? A new *everything*.

With the wedding and honeymoon over, I suddenly ached to make good use of my framed diploma, a Bachelor of Arts in writing. "Wouldn't it be lovely to craft sentences for a living?" I imagined, dreamily.

I had attempted—for one long afternoon—to urge the dream to life. I had heaved our heavy word processor into the back of our slender walk-in closet, my shoulders brushing Jon's dress shirts as I typed away, whipping up a few pages of story before accepting the harsh reality: rent was coming due, and we needed laundry detergent, bread, and eggs. My typed stories would not suffice.

I sighed that day, with no small amount of discouragement, eventually backing out of the closet and away from my dreams.

What transpired in the following days was a flurry of job applications and interviews, leading to my first job offer as a married woman, aged 22. A receptionist I would be.

In a valiant attempt to remain upbeat, I built up this new job in my mind, encouraging myself with the fact that I would at least be working for a Christian company.

My husband brought me back to the moment, asking me, as he drove along, if I was ready for my first day. I squeezed his hand, telling him "Yes!" with a confidence I did not yet feel.

Jon pulled into the parking lot as I gave him a quick farewell kiss. The clock was ticking and he mustn't be late to work. With both hands clutching my purse, lunch bag, water bottle, and a book to read on lunch break, I swished my hip against the passenger door, slamming it shut. Jon smiled and waved goodbye.

I had arrived a few minutes early, with enough time to tuck my lunch in the office refrigerator, straighten my skirt, and run a brush through my humidity-stricken hair. I smiled back at my reflection in the tiny bathroom mirror, applying a touch of lip gloss for good measure, and with a deep breath proceeded to the front desk.

Mandy, the woman who had interviewed me, breezed in with a kind: "Welcome aboard! I'll be right back!"

I smiled and asked God to help me on my first day. I examined my tiny workspace, sat down in the swivel chair, and bent to examine the contents of the lowest desk drawer.

The bell on the front door jingled, and before I could sit fully upright, I heard: "Attention!"

It was shouted military-style, and my heart started racing.

Before me stood a 60-something-year-old man, with squinty eyes magnified by enormous glasses. He was glaring.

"Who are you, young lady?" he bellowed.

I spoke my name and felt my face grow hot under such scrutiny.

"I cannot keep all of you girls straight—you come and go like the wind." His untamed eyebrows furrowed. "My name is Mr. Jackson."

I had not a clue what he meant by "all of you girls," but I knew one thing for certain: it could not be good.

"Dad!" Mandy returned from her office. "Are you scaring our new receptionist?"

She looked at me and winked. I had enjoyed my interview process with her, and she seemed kind. Was this man actually her father?

"Train her right," he shouted. "There's plenty of work to be done around here, and we cannot have anyone wasting God's time." He glared at me again.

"The last girl, Suzy, wasn't it? Or Sandy? I can't remember. She strolled in just on time each day, and I say if you are not 15 minutes early, you are late, so—"

"Dad," Mandy interrupted, "your coffee is in my office. You leave the training to me." She yanked his arm and I was left to wonder what had just happened.

I glanced upward at the office clock, wondering how the rest of the day would unfold.

In those early weeks, I teared up on lunch break, not knowing how this job had turned into such a heartbreak. I cried again as I stirred dinner on the stovetop at home. The one balm was the satisfaction of depositing my small paychecks, thankful to help pay our bills.

Mr. Jackson remained a dark and mighty presence, a force to behold. He barked on the daily—rude and sharp in speech to the handful of employees in the office. On too many days his bark turned into a roar. Nothing was ever right, at least in his mind. The general pulse of the office was akin to stepping over and around tripwires—employees forced to creep and tiptoe, tense and uncertain as to exactly when the bomb might explode.

The office atmosphere pressed in and hovered, choking us with dark negativity. The office blinds were yanked tightly shut, as Mr. Jackson proved miserly, skimping on air-conditioning and not allowing so much as a speck of sunlight to shine inside the old building. He dubbed these as good stewardship measures, squeezing every penny from the company budget in order to fund more missionary work overseas.

Who could argue without sounding perfectly heartless?

And yet didn't a Christ-like attitude mean loving your neighbor? And as employees were we not Mr. Jackson's neighbors? Neighbors left anxious and wanting. The office vibe was unsettling, stingy, harsh.

There was one week during my employment when Mr. Jackson went away to oversee a church missions' building project. Work proved both relaxing and fruitful in his absence, far more productive as the atmosphere warmed.

As our stress levels plummeted, one employee, in a burst of courage, dared to turn the chintzy blinds upward, allowing the sparkling sunshine to flood in and brighten the office—and revealing layers of dust and fingerprint smudges on the outdated wood cabinets. We remedied that with a bucket of scalding soapy water, scrubbing away all remnants of grime. Our spirits lifted, feeling free to work happily. It was a jolly week.

But as soon as Mr. Jackson returned, the sunlight faded as he yanked the blinds shut, complaining about electric bills and questioning our intent: "Have you forgotten those poverty-stricken people overseas?"

It was a confusing time.

I grew quietly sad, my stomach in knots, exhaling with relief when Friday evenings rolled around.

Quitting seemed unimaginable, as we were just starting out as husband and wife. And soon we were dealt another financial blow, as my husband's jaw began to ache. A trip to the dentist ended with the doctor announcing that all four wisdom teeth must be extracted. Immediately. During the same week we received a notice that the first payments of both our student loans were coming due.

While putting forth a brave face, I was quietly, quietly, sinking. Life had grown octopus tentacles, squeezing and pulling me beneath the ocean's waves. The waters were frigid—and as I plunged beneath, yanked downward by concerns, my lungs filled with pressure. I was frightened.

It was growing increasingly difficult to soldier on, walking into and surviving those brutal spaces—a simple receptionist job, made miserable because of one harsh boss. I was no stranger to hard work or correction, as I had worked plenty of jobs throughout high school and college. I was accustomed to bosses explaining protocol and correcting me as needed.

This was not that.

Mr. Jackson, a Christian man, was filled with an insatiable hunger to control, to destroy, to hurl flaming darts at every person in his wake.

I see it clearly now in a way I could not at the time. I was so young, so eager to please, trying terribly hard to get marriage and home-keeping and bills *just right*. I was hard on myself when I perhaps should have been gentle, as married life was so new.

Also?

I embraced a false notion that a boss, especially a Christian boss, was always in the *right*.

And in this, I was wrong.

I never should have stayed employed at such a place.

But I did, for four tedious months.

And then one day, after Mr. Jackson had exploded yet again, storming out of the office in a huff, I knew that the end had come. I stood up from my desk, crossed the hallway, and softly knocked on the office manager's door. I took one look at her composed face and began to sob. She listened with kind eyes, and handed me a tissue.

"He is too cruel. I don't think I can stay," I blubbered.

She nodded. "Kristin, we have gone through so many receptionists." She sighed and glanced at her desk calendar. "Actually, through so many employees. You have stayed far longer than most."

I gave her my two-week notice, and she understood.

When I told Jon that evening, he was fully supportive and deeply empathetic. "We will find a better job for you."

I heard the gentleness in his words.

In an act of faith, we splurged that night, splitting a giant steak sub on four-grained Italian, later enjoying a movie at the local theater, sipping icy Dr. Peppers and holding hands.

The following morning, I began sending out resumes all over again.

Several weeks later I was hired as a receptionist for an air-conditioning company. Rose, the president's secretary, interviewed me. I liked her immensely, but I had been burned once. My optimism was under a hidden lock and key, tempered by recent history.

On the upside, Jon and I had been gifted a car—an ancient station wagon, sporting cranberry vinyl seats and chipped wood paneling. But I was simply grateful to have my own set of wheels—a first for me. Now Jon would not have to drop me off, and we could have a bit more time for breakfast on weekday mornings.

I intentionally arrived 15 minutes early on my first day. Stepping inside, I noticed that the offices were brightly lit, cheerful, and tastefully furnished. There were solid cherry wood tables and desks and bookcases, pretty lamps and bowls of peppermints, light walls and wooden blinds, opened to invite natural light inside—revealing a dust free space. Soft area rugs carpeted the shiny tiled floors, and the air felt fresh, alive, and welcoming.

Rose arrived moments after I did, a smiling and attractive 60-something-year-old woman. Her open-toed pumps clicked daintily on the squeaky clean hallway tile as I followed her to her office to sign the final bit of paperwork.

"Kristin, stay here for just a moment, Dearie. I would like you to meet Mr. Matthews, our President," said Rose afterwards.

My heart jolted as I remembered Mr. Jackson.

Just then a grandfatherly man, clean cut and wearing a fine suit and expensive cologne, entered the office, carrying an Italian leather briefcase.

Rose made the necessary introductions.

"It is a fine pleasure to meet you, Kristin." Mr. Matthews extended his hand. "Welcome to our company."

He placed his briefcase on the desk. His voice was gentlemanly, kind.

"I trust you will make yourself at home. If you have any questions or concerns, my office door is open, and you are free to speak to Rose, who organizes my appointments."

I nodded and thanked him, and the pit in my stomach relaxed.

⤜

The work proved to be far more intense than that of my previous job: fast-paced with a go, go, go atmosphere. The morning slipped by quickly, and the phone rang incessantly.

Mr. Matthews paused by my desk on his way to a lunch meeting. He smiled and inquired how the day had gone so far.

"Good," I said, and meant it.

"Well, I was in the hallway, and I overheard you talking to a customer. I appreciate your friendly words to him. That is how we do business here. Rose is confident that you are the person for the job, and I trust her."

"Thank you," I said, relieved.

He waved and left for lunch.

A few minutes later another client phoned, asking for Mr. Matthews. I sent the call directly to voicemail, given that he was still at lunch, and Rose, although at her desk, was likewise on break, and had requested no interruptions.

Soon, I heard the dainty click of Rose's heels as she approached my desk, telling me that certain clients must *never* be sent to voicemail. She handed me the list.

"These five must always speak to Mr. Matthews, or myself, or to one of the project managers upstairs. Never ever send to voicemail, ok?"

I apologized and nodded, feeling my insides twist, wondering if Mr. Matthews would become unhinged.

Instead, he soon returned and greeted me calmly and directly, saying, "Rose told me that you sent Jim to voicemail. I apologize that we did not explain that to you this morning."

What was this? He was apologizing to me?

"No worries. I know you will always remember from this point forward. This is terribly important, however. He is our largest client and does not tolerate voicemail well."

Mr. Matthews nodded and smiled.

"I am so sorry," I said. "It won't happen again."

He waved his hand. "It's no trouble. Now you know. I am quite certain that this front office is in capable hands. Oh. And one other thing. Rose told me that you and your husband are new to the area?"

I nodded.

"Here is a card for you both. My wife and I would like to invite you to our church if you haven't found one yet."

Soft correction. The soothing balm of Christ.

~~~

"How was it?" Jon hugged me at day's end, studying my face for signs as I chopped parsley, urging it down the cutting board by way of chef's knife and then stirring it into the simmering sauce.

"It was busy but good!" I felt myself grinning. "The president, Mr. Matthews, is the opposite of Mr. Jackson."

"Really?" Jon's eyebrows rose. "What's he like?"

I thought for a moment.

"Gentle," I said.

~~~

There is nothing stronger in the world than gentleness. (Han Suyin)

~~~

Mr. Jackson and Mr. Matthews were Christian men. Both were churchgoers, and both had been entrusted with authority, serving as founder and president of their companies.

People worked beneath them, for them, and answered directly to them.

But Mr. Jackson, who led and corrected with harshness, was left with exhausted, overworked, and skittish employees—men and women who wilted under his verbal brutality and cutting leadership. Few lasted, and the high turnover rate led to ineffective operations.

Mr. Matthews' turnover rate was unusually low. When I accepted the position, the former receptionist had been employed for many years, and left only to retire. Employees stood tall and worked hard, respecting Mr. Matthews' strong, gentle leadership—a quality which yielded robust production by loyal workers.

He rebuked and restored us in the Galatians 6:1 spirit: "Brothers, if anyone is caught in any transgression, you who are spiritual should restore him in a spirit of gentleness. Keep watch on yourself, lest you too be tempted."

In a company as large as his, Mr. Matthews had his fair share of employee issues to confront. Yet I never once heard him raise his voice. People heeded his admonishments, longing to do good by this man.

It often seems as though gentleness is a misunderstood fruit of the spirit, beheld as somewhat weak, wishy-washy, and unattractive. Nothing could be further from the truth. Scripture tells us that God himself is gentle.

[God] will tend his flock like a shepherd;
he will gather the lambs in his arms;

> *he will carry them in his bosom,*
> *And gently lead those that are with young.*
> *(Isaiah 40:11)*

Lest we think such language indicates a lack of strength, pay attention to Zephaniah 3:17:

> *The LORD your God is in your midst,*
> *a mighty one who will save;*
> *he will rejoice over you with gladness;*
> *he will quiet you by his love;*
> *he will exult over you with loud singing.*

Notice the contrast of strength and tenderness. Our heavenly Father is mighty and all-powerful to save us, while also rejoicing and singing over our feeble frames, quieting us by his love. This verse evokes a beautiful portrait of a tender parent, rocking and sweetly hushing their infant—yet all the while, holding their little one safe, secure, and protected.

God's gentleness is matched by his strength. These qualities meet as friends, not opponents. And we see this most clearly displayed in his Son, Jesus.

Jesus Christ is a gentle leader, into whose hands we can entrust ourselves:

> *Come to me, all who labor and are heavy laden, and*
> *I will give you rest. Take my yoke upon you, and*
> *learn from me, for I am gentle and lowly in heart,*
> *and you will find rest for your souls. For my yoke is*
> *easy, and my burden is light. (Matthew 11:28-30)*

Again, don't confuse Christ's gentle nature with sinful passivity. It is nothing like that. Nor is his gentleness ever condoning of sin. He corrects in a way that is mindful not to break a bruised reed, nor quench a smoldering wick (Matthew 12:20).

Christ was gentle with hurting people—those who were weak but not irreparable. This was displayed when the Pharisees brought an adulterous woman before Jesus, saying:

> *"Teacher, this woman has been caught in the act of adultery. Now in the Law, Moses commanded us to stone such women. So what do you say?" This they said to test him, that they might have some charge to bring against him. Jesus bent down and wrote with his finger on the ground. And as they continued to ask him, he stood up and said to them, "Let him who is without sin among you be the first to throw a stone at her." And once more he bent down and wrote on the ground. But when they heard it, they went away one by one, beginning with the older ones, and Jesus was left alone with the woman standing before him. Jesus stood up and said to her, "Woman, where are they? Has no one condemned you?" She said, "No one, Lord." And Jesus said, "Neither do I condemn you; go, and from now on sin no more."*
>
> *(John 8:4-11)*

Gentleness is truth, seasoned with tender grace.

Jesus was gentle with this adulterous woman, a bruised reed who must have been terrified, believing that she was about to die. Of course, she needed to be corrected with truth, given her sin. Which is why Jesus said, *Go and sin no more.* Tender grace!

But he did not condemn her, and neither—by the end of the story—did the accusatory Pharisees.

Why? They had been adamant that she required a stoning. *Guilty! Guilty!* They had cried, fingers pointing as they dropped her in front of Jesus.

Although the text does not elaborate, I am left imagining that as Jesus knelt down, scratching script in the sand, he was spelling out the sins of each accuser, calling them to examine their specific wrongdoings. Might the words of truth spun in the sand have been made visible to their eyes only?

This would have been shattering, convicting, and enough to make them leave, one by one.

And yet Jesus' method, even toward the legalistic Pharisees, was truthful and gentle. He could have shouted their sins for all to hear but he chose elsewise. These prideful men, so quick to point the finger at the adulterous woman, walked away one by one, as the words of the gentle rabbi echoed in their ears: "Let him who is without sin among you be the first to throw a stone at her."

Gentleness is the opposite of domination by condemnation.

Gentle correction is a truth-filled invitation for us to change course. It is helpful to pause and consider: how may I practice receiving correction with a spirit of grateful meekness? And how may I extend gentleness to my family, friends, and coworkers when I am called to correct them?

I was a bruised reed in those early days of marriage—uncertain, feeling weak amid the newness of marriage, acclimating to an unfamiliar part of the country, and figuring out how to manage life as an adult. It was a fragile time.

I look back now and see the gentleness of God in his provision for me—the way he plucked me from a harsh work environment and set me under the umbrella of a godly man, who was gentle with each of his employees. In that contrast I was able to see clearly the strength and power of gentleness over heavy-handedness.

I am asking the Holy Spirit to grow me in his fruit of gentleness. Oftentimes, for those of us who are Christians—who know and love God's word—it is easy to slip into a state of condemnation and harshness with those who need help or correction, whether they are fellow colleagues, loved ones at home, or brothers and sisters in Christ.

Without gentleness, correction may become harsh and critical, spoken from a place of frustration. There is another better way: the way of Christ Jesus, the way of God. The 2 Timothy 2:24-25 way:

> *And the Lord's servant must not be quarrelsome but kind to everyone, able to teach, patiently enduring evil, correcting his opponents with gentleness.*

May God be pleased to grow his gentleness in us today.

NINE

Self-Control: A Passionate Restraint

*"For God gave us a spirit not of fear but of power
and love and self-control."*
(2 Timothy 1:7)

The other night I climbed into bed and sighed in relief.

It had been an arduous week of deadlines, meetings, appointments, and chores. Some things were left unfinished, but regardless, it remained an exquisite delight to curl up in a cloud of softened sheets and warm blankets, unwinding from the day's labors.

I stretched and reached toward my nightstand for my Kindle—dear old chum, so full of good stories.

It has taken me many years to learn how to lay aside my day's work in order to rest. But I've learned more and more to see it for what it is: an exercise in self-control.

Practicing restraint—saying "no" to the temptation to do "just one more thing"—is a choice, a determined moderation. It is a decision to trust God by ceasing. Choosing to rest remains my daily battle for self-control—but it is by no means my first.

I paused on the home screen, perusing my e-reading options, and tapped an old favorite: *Stepping Heavenward* by Elizabeth Prentiss. As my eyes scanned the familiar first paragraph, my mind meandered back in time, to a bright, blue-skied morning, decades ago.

I exited our church following morning worship, shielding my eyes from the stretching summer's sun, and scanning the parking lot for one of my friends.

I had recently graduated from high school, and the future was as bright as the summer's sky. College was on tomorrow's horizon and the possibilities seemed deliciously endless. What would the future hold? I had no clue but soared on the wings of imagination. *Would I get along with my roommate? What other friends would I meet? Was my future husband somewhere on that college campus?*

Time would soon reveal the future's untold mysteries.

A few church women waved me down, flocking about with gift bags full of graduation presents to prepare me for college: soft, luxury towels, 400-thread-count sheets for my dorm bed, pretty headbands, sparkly earrings, scented hand lotions, colorful pens paired with hard-backed journals, plus a basket overflowing with gum and granola bars and brightly wrapped candies.

I had known these women nearly my entire life—or should I say I had known them from afar? They were my mother's and grandmother's contemporaries, not my own. Still, they had adorned my childhood; the wallpaper of my life.

After watching me exclaim over the presents, they began to nudge each other, chitchatting, eyebrows raised. It began innocently enough, discussing the need to pray for so-and-so's daughter who had recently left for college. And then? Their conversation soon turned to tale-bearing, their voices lowered.

"She went on a wild streak, scarcely returning home, running hither and yon with some tattooed boy," one whispered, "prompting her poor, bewildered mother to take to bed, crushed by the indecency of it all."

The women clucked and carried on, hands raised to their hearts, remarking how terribly sorry they felt over the entire conundrum.

This led to the discussion of another student who had failed to send appropriate thank-you notes for the many expensive graduation gifts bestowed upon them. ("So difficult to find! I had to travel to the city and pay a fortune for that item. I even had the clerk wrap it up, and tastefully. And just think! Not a word of thanks!")

And on and on the words trickled, conversation slipping to quicksand.

I slipped away, again scouting for my friend, who was nowhere to be found.

As I meandered across the church parking lot, I heard a soft voice calling.

It was Eleanor.

Eleanor was aged, ladylike, and happy. She was a small woman with large, soulful eyes and a generous smile. I did not know her well but intuited that she was different, and later—much, much later—I would recognize why.

"Hello, dear," she said, holding out a smartly wrapped parcel. "Congratulations on your graduation."

I smiled and tugged off the wrapping paper.

It was a novel: *Stepping Heavenward*, by Elizabeth Prentiss. I had never heard of it.

"Thank you," I said as I gave this tiny woman a hug.

She placed her wrinkled hand on my arm, her nails neatly clipped and coated with clear polish.

"This book is a treasure trove," she said, gently touching the cover. "College will be fun… and full of change. It is best to stay close to God and obey him." Her warm brown eyes drilled into my own.

I nodded.

"I will be praying for you, dear."

Her upturned face was earnest, her words weighty but few. She fluttered her hand in a goodbye and walked away. So did I, suddenly spotting my friend across the parking lot. I called to her and slipped the book inside one of the many other gift bags.

And then I forgot about it for the next five years.

College flew by, as did my wedding. My husband and I had been married for one year when I discovered that I was expecting our first baby. During my first trimester, we moved from one city to another. In the middle of packing and unpacking, I discovered *Stepping Heavenward* peeking at me from the bottom of a box.

I swiftly remembered tender-hearted Eleanor, who had since died, and I felt a pang of regret for not having read the book she had gifted me. Placing it on my nightstand, I was determined to correct such negligence.

After we had settled into our new apartment, I began my new job working as a nanny for a trio of sisters. Following lunchtime, after the girls had settled down to nap and after I had wiped off sticky countertops and swept the crumbs from the floor, I retreated to the plush sofa to relax and read.

I pulled *Stepping Heavenward* from my bag and began chapter one. I could scarcely put it down.

~~~

This book, published in 1869, is told as the journal of Katy, who starts the novel as a moody 16-year-old, born into a loving Christian family. Although the book might seem antiquated to readers today, there is nothing new under the sun, and the reader can catch glimpses of the common battle for self-control that each one of us faces, illustrated by the enduringly captivating character of Katy.

The story begins with her showcasing her temperamental character, bent on gratifying her selfish whims. In contrast, Katy's mother, once upon a time as strong-willed as Katy, is now selfless and sincerely devoted to God, demonstrated by her determined restraint. While she continually prays for Katy to submit to the Lord, she recognizes that the Holy Spirit must lead her daughter.

The subtleties of Katy's passions lead her to grow more dissatisfied and irritable. Such tension is timelessly familiar. Small issues, such as purposefully avoiding chores and sidestepping her mother's requests, soon grow larger and tangled—thorny bushes that ensnare Katy and jab others.

And then? Fairly early in the novel, tragedy strikes, as Katy's father dies unexpectedly.

The following words are from Katy's diary, following the unexpected death of her dear father:

> *Mother spoke to me very seriously today, about controlling myself more. She said she knew this was my first real sorrow, and how hard it was to bear it. But that she was afraid I should become insane some time, if I indulged myself in such passions of grief.*

In the 19th century early death was far more common than today, and her mother's words might at first blush appear harsh. But in the context of the story, Katy's mother is tender and sensitive and deeply concerned about training her daughter to handle grief while practicing self-control.

Despite the serious words, Katy remains fiercely loyal to her mother. Later, they receive visitors into their home during this time of mourning, and one woman informs Katy that Katy's mother seems oddly *firm* rather than *feeling* on the heels of such sorrow.

Katy flares up, later repeating the insult to her mother, who only smiles.

Furious at this insensitive visitor, Katy wonders how anyone could insult her poor mother after such a terrible loss and her irritation grows when her mother chooses not to respond in kind. How she wishes her mother would explode, and when she remains self-controlled Katy grows hot.

> *"Dear Katy," said Mother, "it is not my object in life to make people like me."*

As the novel continues, Katy grows into a young woman. It is only after much struggle and suffering, the pain of broken friendships and even a broken engagement that Katy surrenders herself to Christ, and begins to slowly mature. The snail-paced growth of self-control painted in this story rings true. Its progression takes time and diligence and is not without setbacks.

Stepping Heavenward spans decades of Katy's life, allowing the reader to observe her self-discipline increasing. The book opens with a teenage girl indulging in frivolous speech, a quick temper, self-pity, and a lack of discipline, and ends with a heart softly transformed. From chrysalis to butterfly, Katy blooms in Christ-likeness. The change is exquisite.

As my first pregnancy progressed, I read and re-read *Stepping Heavenward.* I considered the kind woman who gifted me the book, Eleanor, and saw the ways in which she was like Katy's mother. I began to remember how she had practiced self-control by avoiding gossip—instead choosing wise, care-filled words. She resisted expensive purchases on her limited income and expected nothing back from her humble graduation gifts.

I, however, caught more glimpses of myself in the young Katy. This distressed me. I longed to be a good wife and soon-to-be mother, but my self-discipline lacked muscle. *Were my sharp words of retort toward another person God-pleasing, and showing restraint? Did I really need to buy another sweater, another palette of eye shadow, another set of lush towels? Was I willing to show self-control by ceasing to work in order to rest?*

I wanted to learn more about Elizabeth Prentiss, the author of *Stepping Heavenward*, and began to do a little bit of digging. I quickly discovered that many others had been wonderfully impacted by her writings. In fact, during my research, the same name kept reappearing: *Elisabeth Elliot.*

One Saturday I buckled the seatbelt over my protruding belly and made my way to the library, borrowing several Elisabeth Elliot books, which I quickly devoured. This woman—whose first husband, Jim Elliot, was murdered as a missionary in South America—penned stories of her life, and what she knew of God from Scripture.

What a tenacious woman of faith, brimming with self-control!

As a young woman, her passion and deep love for her future husband had remained tempered and self-controlled until marriage.

Her love for delicious food? That was tamed by adhering to appropriate portions.

Her demanding to-do list? That was managed with the aid of structured, meticulous cleaning regimes and specified hours set aside for writing and speaking—ensuring that her house remained orderly while her work deadlines were faithfully met.

She had been twice widowed, losing her second husband to a fast and angry cancer. She had determined to suffer well, doggedly resisting all self-pity, while instead pressing into self-control, trusting in the sovereignty of God.

Restraint permeated her entire existence.

The more I read, the more I wanted to be just like her, and pronto.

But self-control is rarely a rapidly built shelter. It is a slow work, one brick pressed on top of another until a godly house is built. The Christian's self-control is a *practiced* relinquishment—snuffing out fleshly desires while pressing into the Holy Spirit's promptings, in order to please God.

I noticed the distinct way in which Elisabeth Elliot quoted Scripture. It was as though she was bowing low in obedience, verses rolling through her mind and off her tongue, her speech seasoned with God's word. The entire scope left me breathless—mesmerized. Her self-control was a strong and passionate restraint—a joyful, winsome, and willful "yes" to God.

This being said, it was comforting to learn that such self-control was not her natural disposition. By her own admission, and much like *Stepping Heavenward*'s Katy, Elisabeth had once been a highly opinionated, stubborn girl who excelled at debating anyone and everyone. As she was admonished and disciplined by her Christian parents, and again by her teachers at a boarding school, she learned to willfully surrender her will to Christ. It was a long process, but she matured, little by little.

The more I read her books and listened to her radio program, the more I found myself opening my own Bible. Like a gold digger sifting through sand, I unearthed nuggets of treasure as I read along. And here is what I discovered: the path to growing self-control in every area of life hinges on pressing into 2 Timothy 1:7:

> *For God gave us a spirit not of fear but of power and love and self-control.*

If our hearts have truly been transformed from the chains of darkness to the freedom of light, we will hunger for, rather than fear, obedience. God has given his children, through the power of the Holy Spirit, self-control. Like a good soldier, we must dutifully fight for self-control, this passionate restraint. As the pastor Martyn Lloyd-Jones wrote, "Discipline is an absolute essential in an army; it is one of the most important things of all. If an army is not disciplined it is already defeated, it becomes a rabble" (*The Christian Soldier*, Banner of Truth Trust, 1977, p 101).

The concept is simple, just not easy.

⌒

As Christians, we practice the beauty of restraint not for restraint's sake, but out of love for God through the empowerment of the Holy Spirit. As Titus 2:11-14 reminds us, it is "the grace of God" that teaches us to renounce worldly passions in favor of "self-controlled, upright, and godly lives." Jesus died so that we might live!

This is not a bootstrap pulling contest—manufacturing a quick, easy result in our own strength, but rather a chosen act of obedience, fueled by prayer and Scripture feasting, and done from a heart bursting with love for God.

Those three dear women—Eleanor, Elizabeth Prentiss, and Elisabeth Elliot—cast long shadows of influence over me, offering me cool shade in the heat of life. They were women cut from the same cloth, content to be different from the rest of the world. *It was not their object in life to make people like them.*

Their aim?

To please God.

And isn't that the secret of self-control? To take every tiny thought captive—before it morphs into action? Seeking not to please oneself or others, but stretching higher, through wise restraint, aiming only to please God?

Perhaps the most magnificent display of self-control in all of Scripture is that of Jesus. Immediately after he is baptized by John the Baptist, Jesus is intentionally led into the wilderness by the Holy Spirit, so that he may be tempted by Satan.

> *Then Jesus was led up by the Spirit into the wilderness to be tempted by the devil. And after fasting forty days and forty nights, he was hungry. And the tempter came and said to him, "If you are the Son of God, command these stones to become loaves of bread." But he answered, "It is written,*

*"'Man shall not live by bread alone, but by every
word that comes from the mouth of God.'"*

*Then the devil took him to the holy city and set him
on the pinnacle of the temple and said to him, "If you
are the Son of God, throw yourself down, for it is
written,*

"'He will command his angels concerning you,'

and

*"'On their hands they will bear you up,
lest you strike your foot against a stone.'"*

*Jesus said to him, "Again it is written, 'You shall not
put the Lord your God to the test.'" Again, the devil
took him to a very high mountain and showed him
all the kingdoms of the world and their glory. And he
said to him, "All these I will give you if you will fall
down and worship me." Then Jesus said to him, "Be
gone, Satan! For it is written,*

*"'You shall worship the Lord your God
and him only shall you serve.'"*

*Then the devil left him, and behold, angels came and
were ministering to him. (Matthew 4:1-11)*

Jesus demonstrated the beauty of self-control. How did
Jesus practice such restraint? The Scriptures give us the
answers, with stunning clarity. This is a superb roadmap

for us to follow, as we strengthen our roots, growing spiritual fruit of self-control.

Jesus was aware. Jesus did not walk into this situation unwittingly, only to be blindsided by the devil. He went into the wilderness in order "to be tempted." Although not explicit in this passage, Scripture as a whole is clear: Jesus, our suffering Savior, knew that a time of painful testing would come during his earthly ministry. Yet this was for our sake: because of his temptation at the hand of Satan, Jesus is able to sympathize with our weaknesses when we are tempted—and we certainly will be (Hebrews 2:18; Hebrews 4:15; Isaiah 53:3). As Christians, it is important for each of us to remain aware that we, like Christ, will also face strong enticements to sin. It is not God who tempts us, but our own fleshly desires (James 1:13-14).

Jesus was Spirit-led. Jesus followed the Spirit into the wilderness. Scripture tells us he was led, not forced. He hungered to do the will of his Father, and therefore eagerly followed the Holy Spirit.

Jesus was prepared. Jesus prepared his soul by going away to the wilderness, spending time alone with God in prayer. He did not rush his preparation, but remained self-controlled, fasting and communing with God for 40 days, in order to be ready for temptation.

Jesus was strengthened. Christ was strengthened by feasting on the word—each temptation turned aside by reciting what "is written" in Scripture (Matthew 4, 7, 10). Think of how physically hungry he must have been after 40 days without food. But the word of God was enough to sustain him spiritually.

Jesus was firmly rooted. Jesus was not baited, nor tugged away by Satan. He was so deeply rooted in the will of God that the promptings of the Spirit guided him in his self-controlled responses. Jesus took every temptation captive, battling the devil with the sword of Scripture.

It was a battle he won. Every single time.

Indeed, this passage doesn't primarily tell *us* what to *do*; it celebrates what *Jesus* has *done*. Jesus' self-control and obedience—his triumph over Satan—was done on our behalf. It meant that on the cross, he could offer up his sinless life—his spotless record of righteousness—for our sake. What good news for each one of us, children of God who regularly fail much less intense testing. We are more like the Old Testament children of Israel in the wilderness, who grumbled and disobeyed and fell flat.

It gets even better. The Son of Man's ultimate defeat of Satan now allows us, once and for all time, to be indwelled and guided by the same Holy Spirit who filled him, despite our ongoing sins and weaknesses.

We may be firmly rooted because of Christ's perfect self-control. His faithfulness and his power are now ours.

Perhaps you are thinking: I *want* to choose self-control, but I am not Jesus, and I certainly cannot abandon my life and enter the wilderness for 40 days without food.

May I suggest starting small?

Choose one area and begin to practice restraint.

Do you gossip?

If so, become *aware* of your words. *Follow the Holy Spirit* in obedience, *preparing* yourself by praying to God to help you restrain ungodly speech. Make sticky notes or index cards, *strengthening your soul* with Bible verses exhorting the practice of kind words that build up versus unkind words that tear down. Whisper to yourself Jesus' own words: "It is written." *Be firmly rooted* in the Lord's love for you, taking every thought captive before you speak.

Satan attacks what he knows to be our weaknesses, stirring up fleshly desires. Be alert to his schemes. Maybe your sinful proclivity bends toward lust, or food, or drink, or racking up credit-card debt. Do you overwork? Or perhaps you are prone to indulging in laziness?

However your lack of self-control manifests, begin small. Be aware and on your guard, turn and follow the Holy Spirit's leading, intentionally preparing yourself for battle through the word which will strengthen you. Stay firmly rooted by taking every thought captive.

Obey in this precise moment, one step at a time. This is not about tomorrow, but today.

Those high school graduation presents I received in the church parking lot all those decades ago are long gone—the oversized towels, scented lotions, and baskets of snacks and their wrappings likely buried somewhere in the depths of a midwestern landfill. As kind and generous such gifts were, it was Eleanor's gift that lives on, surpassing time. Her book, her prayers, and her wisdom in godly restraint presses upon me still—bearing fruit. That one small gift sent me on a quest for God.

A journey of passionate restraint.

REFLECTION
QUESTIONS

Chapter 1: *Love*

1. Whose example of Christ-like love has impacted you?

2. As you reflect on this chapter, what strikes you as especially extravagant about God's love for you?

3. "Consider the day ahead. How could you start giving yourself away for the good of others in some small way?" (p 22).

4. Who do you find particularly costly to love? How does it change your perspective to know that "God sees and treasures such heartfelt sacrifice, however small it is in the world's eyes" (p 26)?

Chapter 2: Joy

1. Whose example of Christ-like joy has impacted you?

2. "It gives me so much joy to know that we saved them," Mrs. Dawson said about the puppies (p 34). Do you typically think of God taking *joy* in saving you? Why or why not? Spend a few moments now imagining him rejoicing over you with loud singing (Zephaniah 3:17).

3. Are there any areas of your heart where you are allowing sulking, complaining, or self-pity to take root? Confess them to the Lord.

4. "Jesus loves me, this I know." In what situations would you like the Spirit to help you to hold onto this truth, so that you may rejoice? Speak to him about them now.

Chapter 3: Peace

1. When have you known the Spirit's peace in the midst of a "storm"?

2. What are the "What ifs?" that threaten to rob you of peace in the present time? Write them down and speak to the Lord about them.

3. For each "What if?", think of a corresponding "fear not" from God's word. (How might Jesus complete the sentence: "Fear not for..."?) Write them down and imagine Jesus speaking them to you one by one.

Chapter 4: *Patience*

1. "God often teaches us patience through seasons of inconvenient circumstances, spent with deeply frustrating people" (p 63-64). Have you experienced that to be true in the past?

2. "God has no shortage of eggs, and he stands patiently, arms outstretched, giving you another opportunity" (p 66). How have you seen God's patience toward you?

3. What situations—big or small—tend to try your patience in this present season? Repent of times when you have been impatient—and rejoice that the Spirit has graciously convicted you of sin! Ask him to grow more of the good fruit of patience in your life.

Chapter 5: *Kindness*

1. Do you know someone who is unusually kind? What makes them so? Thank God for them.

2. How have you seen God's kindness to you? Reflect on that question in terms of your day, your week, your month, and the whole span of your life so far.

3. To whom is the Spirit prompting you to be kind today, and how? What difference does it make to imagine that as you serve "the least of these," you serve Jesus himself (Matthew 25:31-40)?

Chapter 6: Goodness

1. Do you know a "Micah 6:8"-man or woman? How do they reflect the "stained-glass beauty" of Jesus?

2. Which of the three cords of goodness—justice, kindness, humility—are you most prone to neglect? Confess the ways in which you've fallen short.

3. Which of the three cords of goodness have you seen the Spirit growing in your life? Rejoice at this fruit.

4. Read Titus 3:3-7. What reasons for hope and reassurance do you see here, as you think about the area of goodness?

Chapter 7: Faithfulness

1. "God is faithfully stitching all things together for our good" (p 109). In what ways have you discovered that to be true over the years, like Ginny had? What would you say to your younger self to encourage them?

2. Close your eyes and imagine your Christian life as a marathon, like on page 113 What are the conditions for you at the moment? Talk to your Father about what you see. Is there anything that threatens your faithful endurance?

3. Consider the three keys to faithfulness from Hebrews 10:19-25: "Draw near," "Hold fast," and "Stir up one another to love and good works." What is one practical step you'd like to take, praying that the Spirit would use it to help you endure to the finish line?

Chapter 8: Gentleness

1. Whose Christ-like example of gentleness has impacted you? How do they reflect the gentle strength of Jesus?

2. In what ways do you need to grow in gentleness when receiving correction? Ask the Spirit to help you.

3. In what ways do you need to grow in gentleness when giving correction? Ask the Spirit to help you.

4. In addition to John 8:4-11, what other passages come to mind that display Jesus' gentleness?

Chapter 9: Self-Control

1. Where have you seen the Spirit growing the fruit of self-control in your life? Take stock and rejoice!

2. In what areas does your self-control still lack muscle? Choose one, and work through the steps on pages 143-145.
   - *Aware:* Ask the Spirit to make you aware of your sin and show you how he wants you to grow.
   - *Spirit-led:* Ask the Spirit to lead you into obedience in this area.
   - *Prepared:* Think ahead to your day or week. When is this struggle at its sharpest for you? What would responding to temptation with self-control look like in these situations?
   - *Strengthened:* Choose a Bible verse that will help you in this battle, and spend time reflecting on it.
   - *Rooted:* Plan ways in which you will return to this Bible verse throughout your day and week.